ALSO BY GREGORY CURTIS

The Cave Painters
Disarmed

Paris Without Her

Paris Without Her

 A MEMOIR

Gregory Curtis

Alfred A. Knopf   New York   2021

THIS IS A BORZOI BOOK PUBLISHED BY ALFRED A. KNOPF

Copyright © 2021 by Gregory Curtis

All rights reserved. Published in the United States by Alfred A. Knopf, a division of Penguin Random House LLC, New York, and distributed in Canada by Penguin Random House Canada Limited, Toronto.

www.aaknopf.com

Library of Congress Cataloging-in-Publication Data
Names: Curtis, Gregory, [date] author.
Title: Paris without her: a memoir / Gregory Curtis.
Description: First edition. | New York: Alfred A. Knopf, 2021. | "This is a Borzoi book published by Alfred A. Knopf." |
Identifiers: LCCN 2020026090 (print) | LCCN 2020026091 (ebook) | ISBN 9780525657620 (hardcover) | ISBN 9780525657637 (ebook)
Subjects: LCSH: Curtis, Gregory, 1944– | Curtis, Gregory, 1944– Travel—France—Paris. | Curtis, Tracy, 1943–2011—Travel—France—Paris. | Editors—United States— Biography. | Widowers—United States—Biography. | Spouses of cancer patients—United States—Biography. | Spouses—Death— Psychological aspects. | Paris (France)—Description and travel. | Paris (France)—Biography.
Classification: LCC PN4874.C96 A3 2021 (print) | LCC PN4874.C96 (ebook) | DDC 741.6/52092 [B]—dc23
LC record available at https://lccn.loc.gov/2020026090
LC ebook record available at https://lccn.loc.gov/2020026091

Jacket painting by David Meldrum
Jacket design by Jenny Carrow

Manufactured in the United States of America
First Edition

To Liza Richardson, Quentin White, Vivian Potterf, Ben Curtis, Isabella Savage, Jackson Savage, Jesse Ramos, George Potterf, and Sadie Curtis—Tracy's children and grandchildren.

Qui ne sait pas peupler sa solitude, ne sait pas non plus être seul dans une foule affairée.

—Charles Baudelaire, *Le Spleen de Paris*

CONTENTS

PART I

*There Is No Love
Except Love at First Sight*

CHAPTER ONE

The Last Good Year

I remember clearly the first time I saw Tracy. It was on a sunny spring day in 1974 at the shabby offices of *Texas Monthly*, then just one year old. In those days the magazine was in a squat, miserable building at 15th and Guadalupe in Austin, Texas, that was torn down long ago. A staircase from the sidewalk led to the second floor, which the magazine shared with a dental laboratory run by a mysterious, solitary man. He was seldom there during the day, worked irregular hours during the night, and never spoke to any of us at the magazine, ever.

I was sitting at my desk, one among three others in a large room that was the writers' bullpen, when Tracy appeared in the doorway. She was being shown around the office by the publisher, not that there was much to see. Unlike the four of us in the bullpen, she was elegantly dressed and radiantly beautiful, as she would be all her life. She had luminous skin, dark eyes, and luxurious, wavy black hair. I still know precisely what I was thinking at that moment—nothing. I couldn't think. I felt a charged current electrify my brain, and that intense, electric moment would give her power over me forever. I didn't know then that I would marry her, but I did know that I loved her.

And I remember clearly the last time I saw Tracy. It was four in the morning, Friday, January 28, 2011. The chilly winter day had not yet dawned. I was alone with her in her room in a hospice. Her hair was thin and brittle, and her face was slack and pallid as she lay lifeless on her bed. She was three months shy of her sixty-eighth birthday. "Oh, poor darling," I said.

I held her hand and kissed her and sat beside the bed, looking at her intently. During our thirty-five years of marriage, we had always known when one of us was looking at the other, even if our attention was elsewhere. When I felt Tracy's eyes, or when she felt mine, we turned toward each other. Our eyes said everything. But now, of course, as I sat beside her, although she may have known somehow, somewhere, what I was thinking, she did not turn to meet my eyes. Instead, a vast emptiness opened before me.

There was a soft knock at the door. The men from the funeral home had arrived with the hearse.

.   .   .

Tracy had been a defiant smoker. She had started during high school and continued for most of the rest of her life. In 1997, an X-ray revealed a spot in her right lung, and two-thirds of the lung had to be removed. That spot turned out to be a hard little ball of cancer. Since it was so hard and compact, the doctors thought that all the cancer cells had been removed. Maybe they had, maybe they hadn't, but at least Tracy was frightened enough to stop smoking. But her lung cancer returned in 2003. This time we went to the MD Anderson Cancer Center in Houston, an internationally renowned institution whose treatment of cancer is as fine as any in the world. Her doctor was clearly brilliant, but also intense, concentrated, sometimes brusque.

Tracy liked him. She also liked his unflappable, country-girl nurse, who somewhat sweetened his brusque effect. The doctor prescribed a regimen of chemotherapy and radiation treatments that would last six to eight weeks.

Every Monday morning, we drove to Houston, where we had rented an apartment near MD Anderson. We spent most of every day at the hospital until Friday afternoon, when we drove back to Austin for the weekend. Tracy's treatments were painful and debilitating. There were also endless tests and appointments with various doctors, so we spent a lot of time in crowded, dismal waiting rooms until Tracy's name would finally be called. MD Anderson is an immense labyrinth of long, dark hallways leading to banks of elevators and various attached buildings. It was easy to get lost, and we often did.

It was also dismal in the evening at the apartment we had rented. The smell of cooking nauseated Tracy, so I ate out and brought her back a milkshake, which was about the only food she could tolerate. We discovered that one of the cable channels there showed the nightly news from TV5Monde in Paris. We had taken several trips to France together and had become dedicated Francophiles. And we were both committed to learning French, although our progress had been slow. Now we sat together on a couch in the evening and watched the French news faithfully, although we didn't understand much. And—blessed miracle—that summer my alma mater, Rice University, won the College World Series. Neither of us followed college baseball, but we watched the final game, against Stanford, happy to have this unexpected and unlikely diversion from thinking about cancer.

Fortunately, the treatments seemed to be working and were discontinued after six weeks, although we had to return to

Houston for checkups four times a year. Finally, on one happy day in 2007 when we were in the office of her doctor, he said, "You are cancer-free."

Tracy felt not only healthy but liberated. When the chemo and radiation stopped in 2003, at the age of sixty she heroically returned to college for four years to earn a second undergraduate degree so that she could become a licensed interior designer. As part of her degree program, she had been required to take a course called Family Living. Everything about this course— the requirement itself, the droning professor, the expensive and useless textbook—annoyed Tracy. "I've had two husbands," she said. "I've been married over thirty years. I've raised four children. What is it they think I don't know about family living?" But she got her degree and passed the licensing examination and started a business. Since her taste in anything visual was impeccable, and since she was personally gracious and charming, she soon had a number of clients who liked her work and recommended her to others. At last she was making money on her own, something she had always wished for. She was doing well, the children were all doing well, I was doing well, and we were very happy together. That lasted seven years.

For the first eight months, 2010 was a particularly good year. In April, our daughter, Vivian, got married. Her husband, Jason, was a funny, happy, brilliant electrical engineer. Our son, Ben, performed the ceremony that Vivian and Jason had written. Friends of ours and theirs had come from all across the country. When the band began, I danced with the bride and Tracy danced with the groom, and then we traded partners and everyone started dancing. At one point, the aggressive wife of one of our friends was standing so close to a man other than her husband that he was trapped against the wall and was squirming to get away. It was comical. I looked for Tracy just as she was looking for me. When our eyes met, we both began smiling like conspirators.

That summer, we spent four weeks on Cape Cod. I conducted seminars at the Norman Mailer Writers Colony, which in those days met at Mailer's looming, creaky, book-stuffed, strangely furnished house in Provincetown. Tracy and I were provided with a comfortable apartment on the top floor of a blue wooden house on Commercial Street. There was a glorious flower garden in the front yard. From the windows in our apartment, we could look down on the garden or out across the bay, where sometimes black thunderheads loomed in the night sky and spikes of lightning flashed over the ocean.

A couple who had been dear friends for many years also spent summers on the Cape. We made friends there through them, so those four weeks were filled with pleasant walks and cookouts on the beach and much laughter. Everything was idyllic except that, all the while, Tracy was sometimes bothered by discomfort around her stomach and kidneys, which she thought was indigestion. When we returned to Austin in mid-August, she went to see our general practitioner. He sent her to get chest X-rays. After seeing her film, he called us. He had made an appointment for Tracy at a specialized clinic the next day, which was a Saturday. After more X-rays and an examination, the doctor at the clinic told us we needed to check Tracy into MD Anderson in Houston *that very day*. He would call and get her admitted. Our pleasant summer was over. She had pancreatic cancer.

We quickly packed some bags and glumly, apprehensively, drove to Houston. At MD Anderson, everything was depressingly familiar after our time there seven years earlier—the

steep, narrow parking lot, the efficient women at the registration desk, the maze of hallways filled with really sick, pallid,
despairing patients sitting in wheelchairs or lying on gurneys.
Finally, we found Tracy's small room, with an array of moni-
tors on wheels. She changed into a hospital gown and reluctantly climbed into the stiff, sanitary sheets of a metal hospital
bed. A nurse snapped the bars on the sides of the bed into place
and put a needle in Tracy's forearm in order to start a drip.

She needed to have a surgery known as the Whipple procedure, which would remove the cancer at the head of her pancreas as well as some of the small intestine, the gallbladder, and
the bile duct. But Tracy couldn't have this surgery, because
the malignant tumor in her pancreas was wrapped around an
artery. Her treatment began with some chemotherapy intended
to shrink the tumor, but it was soon discontinued because the
chemo made her so sick.

I rented a motel room nearby without knowing how long
we would be in Houston. At the hospital, Tracy lay in her bed,
dozing off and on, while listening through headphones to a
reading of *The Count of Monte Cristo*. I was distraught to see her
once again in a hospital bed with a needle in her arm and a drip
going, as she had been so often seven years ago. She looked thin
and spiritless. I did not tell her about a phone call I had received
the second afternoon she was in the hospital.

A friend who was involved in raising money for MD
Anderson arranged for me to receive a call from a man who
had recently survived pancreatic cancer. I took the call sitting
in Houston's intense August heat, on a bench outside the hospital. It was one of the rare times I left Tracy's room, because
the doctors attending to her arrived unpredictably and I didn't
want to be gone when they made an appearance. The man who

called had been lucky: the location of his tumor had permitted the Whipple procedure. Few patients with pancreatic cancer are that lucky. He said that he thought the best way to be helpful to me was to be blunt. "You should be prepared," he warned me, "because, if she can't have that surgery, she's going to die. And you should know that she could die even if they *can* do the Whipple surgery." That was certainly blunt, but it also turned out to be quite helpful. I thought of his words often during the coming weeks, when none of the medical staff attending to Tracy—not nurses, not doctors, not administrators—ever spoke to either of us that clearly.

The doctors who examined Tracy agreed that they needed to put in a stent. The pancreas is an organ about the size of a corncob that sits behind the stomach, where it is surrounded by the small intestine, the liver, and the spleen. It can even look like a corncob, or, more often, like a tuber of some exotic kind. It helps digest food and regulate blood sugar. Cancer blocks the pancreas so that food can't get through as it should. That was why Tracy kept feeling as if she had indigestion while we were on Cape Cod. A stent is a small tube with a very narrow diameter. Properly placed, it allows food to pass through the pancreas once again. The stent cannot stay in place permanently, but in theory it allows the patient to survive while other treatments, such as drugs, chemotherapy, and radiation, set out to destroy the cancer.

But placing the stent properly in Tracy would not be easy. During the procedure, the stent is forced down the patient's throat, through the esophagus and stomach, to the pancreas. All the chemo and radiation Tracy had endured in 2003 had shrunk her esophagus and made it somewhat brittle, or at any rate less flexible. If her esophagus were to be ripped open, she

would die from that rather than from the cancer. A doctor asked
her if she wanted to take that chance.

"Yes," she said calmly.

I didn't question her decision. It did seem to be her only
chance. The doctors also said that this cancer was a completely
separate occurrence and wasn't related to her lung cancer seven
years ago. Maybe so, and maybe not. I wasn't certain, but didn't
know nearly enough to question the doctors. Besides, smoking is associated with pancreatic cancer as well as lung cancer.
And Tracy's father had died from the same disease. She had
quit smoking, but there had been years and years when she did
smoke, and perhaps she had inherited a susceptibility to the disease as well. Or perhaps she just had bad luck. The origin of
her cancer hardly mattered now. All that mattered was that she
had it.

There was one surgeon at the hospital who specialized
in putting in stents, so the operation had to wait a day or so
before he could fit Tracy into his schedule. He came by her
room one afternoon. He was a tall country boy, wearing a stiff
tie whose color and pattern were much at odds with the color
and pattern of his suit. He was shy and awkward and looked
away rather than meeting your gaze. He had long, thin fingers
that he waved as he talked. He asked a few questions, looked
at her X-rays, and felt her methodically from her throat down
her esophagus to her stomach, and then, more slowly, back up
again. "This will be all right," he said finally, and scheduled the
procedure for the following morning.

The operation went as well as it could, and Tracy had her
stent, but her throat was so raw that ice cream was all she could
eat. In a few days, though, she was much better. The drip was

removed and she was discharged from the hospital. That was heartening for us both. But before we left Houston, we had seen the doctor who would supervise her continuing treatments. The three of us met in his office. In a completely neutral tone, he said that the only hope now, as it had been all along, was to shrink the tumor enough for the Whipple procedure to become possible. Although Tracy couldn't tolerate chemo any longer, perhaps radiation alone would shrink the tumor. Even if the radiation shrank it only slightly, that would make whatever time she had left easier for her. Or, as the doctor mentioned in a flat tone, the radiation could have no effect on the tumor whatsoever. Tracy was sitting alone on his examining table with a hospital gown gathered around her and a stony look on her face. "I'm one tough lady" was all she said.

So began several months when, once again, we drove three hours to Houston Monday morning and returned to Austin Friday afternoon. Each morning, a technician at the hospital scalded Tracy's skin and some of her internal organs with focused radiation for about fifteen minutes. Fortunately, in November and early December, a cousin of Tracy's who was traveling extensively let us stay in her large condominium, not far from MD Anderson. It was on the top floor of a high-rise with a view all around. In the night, after a torturous day at the hospital, it was comforting to look down on Houston, which seemed serenely peaceful as its lights glowed below us in the darkness.

The treatments ended in early December, but Tracy wasn't better. She saw doctors in Austin, which had little effect. She was with all the family during Christmas and attended our annual New Year's Eve party with friends for half an hour or so. As days in January went by, it became clear that hospice was the best place for her now, and ten days after she was admitted to the hospice, she died there.

.   .   .

Her funeral was on a gray, cold, bitter Wednesday morning. The four children and I sat together in a front pew of an Episcopal church. There were two daughters from her first marriage, and a daughter and a son from ours. The three daughters were married, so their husbands were there, too, as well as a granddaughter and two grandsons. I had written Tracy's eulogy the night before. I was surprised that I was able to write her eulogy quickly and without much fumbling for the right words. At the time, I did not yet understand that what I was feeling then was sadness, not grief. Grief would not come until a week or two later, and after arriving once, it would come again and again. I could manage sadness, but I was helpless against grief.

The minister at the Episcopal church officiated at the service. After making some preliminary comments, he called me to the pulpit to speak. "She didn't like driving on flyovers or across bridges," my eulogy began, "but otherwise there was nothing she was afraid of." I told the children directly that she knew they loved her, and they should take comfort from that. I also said: "She could see clearly. I think it was her great gift. She could see clearly what was there before her. It sounds simple, but I think it is the most difficult thing in the world to do. And she did it naturally, instinctively. She could look at someone, and she knew. She could look at a work of art, and she knew. She could look at a sofa, and she knew."

There was more, including a poem. After I finished, I sat back down beside the children, and the minister spoke. I had met him a few years before, at a lecture I had given at the church, and hadn't liked him much. He hadn't known Tracy well and hadn't known our family at all, but he had definitely been a comfort to her in the final weeks of her illness. I was grateful for that, and didn't mind that he wanted to speak. But he began by saying that Tracy was afraid of dying, which contradicted what I had just said, and which I thought then, and still think now, was not true. She didn't want to die, but that's not the same thing as being afraid. He spoke on, but I was annoyed and tuned him out. The next thing I remember is walking out of the church and seeing Rosie, our maid, in a pew at the back, sobbing uncontrollably. Tracy had hired Rosie fifteen years earlier. She was just seventeen then, newly arrived from Nicaragua, and didn't speak a single word of English. Now she was a naturalized citizen, married, and the mother of three children. "Como mi madre," she wailed. "Como mi madre."

Next I remember sitting in the back of a limousine, waiting for the procession to the cemetery to begin. Behind a darkly tinted window, I watched our friends solemnly leaving the church. I was surprised and strangely touched when I saw that our accountants had come to the service. They hardly knew her. I remember nothing of the interment except embracing her first husband and then embracing a colleague who had driven from Houston to be there. And then I wanted our son, Ben, near me in the limo when it was over.

There was a nice reception afterward, in the common room on the first floor of our condominium. Some friends had come to the funeral from far places, which was comforting. And the four children were there, of course, as well as some of their friends. There was good food and good wine, thanks to two of Tracy's closest friends, who had put the event together for me. People ate and talked and hugged and then, after an hour or so, drifted away. The children and I all embraced each other as they left with their families. At the end of the afternoon, I found myself alone in my apartment with a plate of food I had saved from the reception for dinner.

The three girls had gone through Tracy's things for me. They kept jewelry and mementos but gave all her clothes to charity, or so I assume—I realize now that I don't really know what they did with her clothes. My own clothes hung in half-empty closets in the bedroom. Tracy and I always had a drink before dinner, with music playing, so I put on some music and had a drink.

Despite the music, I felt a deafening silence. In the next few days, I switched to sleeping on Tracy's side of the bed and abandoned my bathroom to take over hers, which was larger and nicer. At least, I thought so. She had never gotten over her annoyance that the washer and dryer were there. I made no changes in our condominium. None. Tracy had redesigned the place completely when we bought it, and I didn't want anything to change.

During the weeks that followed, I found that music, which I had loved all my life, couldn't fill the silence that descended in the evenings. Instead of listening, I began watching magic-instruction DVDs that I ordered from L&L Publishing in Lake Tahoe, California. Magic had been a hobby of mine for a dozen years or so. It began when Tracy and I were in San Antonio one afternoon, driving north on Broadway, toward the highway back to Austin. I noticed a hulking old house with a sign stretched across the second floor that said "Magic Shop." On an impulse, I pulled over and we went in. I bought a couple of

tricks and a cassette tape called *Easy to Master Card Miracles*.
I became somewhat serious about magic and dedicated time
to learning tricks. I even did some performances at parties for
friends.

Now magic became my solitary mania. I watched the
instructional DVDs week after week and ordered new ones
regularly. I thought of them as presents to myself. It helped
to have someone talking to me and teaching me something at
night, before dinner. I took copious notes that eventually filled
fifteen notebooks. I thought seriously about creating an act
that I would try out at open-mic nights at local comedy clubs,
although I never did.

Occasionally, I went to dinner with friends. I saw my
daughters more frequently, and once a week Ben dropped by
for dinner, which was good for us both. I taught a course at
the University of Texas, and also worked and had an office at
the Harry Ransom Center, the university's special-collections
library. Very conveniently, it is just two blocks away from my
apartment. My appointment was for only two hours a day, but
I stayed in my office until late in the afternoon. I wrote some
magazine articles and book reviews and tried to find a book
to write. I lingered in the afternoons at the Ransom Center,
because I liked my colleagues there and liked being in an atmosphere of writing, research, and learning. So, after days that
were mostly pleasant, I was not usually in a dark mood when
I went home alone and spent evenings with the magic DVDs.
I was surprised when I realized that I wasn't especially lonely. I
didn't become a recluse, but I was definitely private and solitary. Though I didn't want the pattern of these days to be my
life forever, for the moment I didn't really mind and didn't have
any notion of what I might want instead.

I did know that somehow I had to reconcile my life of the last thirty-five years with Tracy with my life ahead without her. Sometimes, in the weeks that followed, as I was drowning in waves of grief, that reconciliation seemed impossible. What should I do? And how could I even begin to do it?

My evenings with the magic DVDs were a pathetic, almost comical substitute for the evenings Tracy and I had shared. But their general good cheer, even though they were only shadows of what had been, were comforting reminders of evenings with her and of good times and of all that we'd shared. Although our marriage was mostly loving and happy, we'd had many arguments in our years together. Some were trivial, but others were wounding and would last for days, or a week, or occasionally even longer. We quarreled about money, sex, children, love, and about nothing. At one time or another, we both threatened leaving and divorcing. There were painful, mocking gibes, claims that the only feeling left was pity or contempt. But I didn't remember all these quarrels, really. Though I knew they had happened, they were dwarfed and suppressed by her absence. I did what I did in the past and said what I said, and so did she. Nevertheless, we stayed together; neither of us wanted to live apart from the other. None of that drama, which was hurtful at the time, bothered me now. None of it even mattered. I wanted to use memories of all our good times to try to reconcile our past together with my future alone. During those evenings alone, as I looked back across the years of our marriage, it became plain to me that our best times and our happiest times and our times of laughter and bliss were the times we spent together in Paris. And before long those memories would draw me to Paris again.

 PART II

The Standing Lion

The Red Coat

As I write this, it is Sunday, February 24, 2019, and I'm back in Paris. The weather is exhilarating—sixty degrees, no wind, and a clear, blue sky. I decided to take a long walk—from my apartment to the Boulevard Saint-Michel, then down the rue Monsieur-le-Prince to the Carrefour de l'Odéon, from there down Boulevard Saint-Germain, and eventually to 44 rue Jacob, where I would visit again the Hôtel d'Angleterre. That was where Tracy and I stayed the first time we visited Paris, in late March 1982. She was thirty-eight and I was thirty-seven. We had been married for almost six and a half years. Neither of us had ever been to Europe before.

We went because the West German government had a program at that time that gave American journalists private tours across Germany. Just the year before, I had been named editor of *Texas Monthly*, and I had been invited to participate. Tracy was not included on the German tour, but we could use my free ticket on Lufthansa and buy her a ticket and go anywhere we pleased during the weeks before my German tour. Tracy's parents came to stay with the children while we were gone.

First we went to Rome. After many delays during our

flight, and a harrowing ride in a cab from the airport to our hotel—the cab driver never slowed down on blind, hillside curves; instead, he honked two or three times and sped on— we arrived at our hotel, the Valadier. We had to rouse the desk clerk from his bed to check in. Our room had a plush, comfortable bed and a bathroom so small that the shower soaked the toilet seat. The desk clerk told us about a restaurant nearby that would still be open. There we had salad and a steaming, spicy pasta, our first European meal. The rest of our time in Rome went smoothly enough after that.

In fact, we were feeling especially close to each other. We knew no one in Rome, we had to find the sights of the city as best we could and explore them together, and the only way we could share our experiences in that moment was to talk with one another. We talked constantly, but entirely about what was happening in the moment. Yes, we thought about the children and our friends, but less than either of us would have expected. The present was so rich with sensations invoked by the wonders around us that it took all our energy to absorb the experiences we were having. It was as if we had no history between us before Rome, and all we knew of one another was what was happening to us now.

One moment in particular united us as never before. We had read what we were certain was good advice about seeing the Sistine Chapel. The guidebook said that there was a "back door" to the Vatican—it took us a few moments to stop laughing after reading that phrase—that opened earlier than the basilica itself. We should be there and enter the moment the back door opened. Then we were to walk down long corridors to the Sistine Chapel without stopping even for a moment to look more closely at any of the countless treasures we would be passing. We followed these instructions scrupulously and arrived at the chapel with only three other people; apparently, we had all read the same guidebook. The chapel was silent and virtually empty. Tracy and I held hands as we slowly walked around, looking up at the ceiling, experiencing it not as two but as one person.

We were there for a long time before deciding to walk back and consider more closely the things we had passed, in particular the Raphael Rooms, which had almost as powerful an effect on us as did the chapel. Then we decided to take one more look before leaving. But when we got to the chapel, it was filled. Since everyone was looking up at the ceiling, people bumped into each other constantly. We didn't want to spoil the visit we had already had, so we left.

. . .

Some close friends, who were seasoned travelers in Italy and France, told us that if we were going from Rome to Paris, we shouldn't fail to make a pilgrimage to eat at Les Frères Troisgros in Roanne. So, when it was time to leave Rome, we flew to Geneva and rented a car. We crossed the border into France, headed toward Roanne, and of course got lost along the way. We didn't realize we were lost until we found ourselves on a narrow gravel road along the side of a hill overlooking a verdant valley. It was a lovely view, but we couldn't be on the right road.

As we rounded a curve, we saw two elderly ladies who were evidently out for a stroll. Digging deep into my memory of my hated French classes at Rice, I rolled down my window and said, "Bonjour, mesdames. La route à Roanne?" They both stared at me bewildered. Neither Tracy nor I knew that

"Roanne" was pronounced rather like the Spanish name Juan, so that it rhymes with "yawn." We were saying "Row-Anne," so the two ladies had no idea which "route" I meant. I was oblivious, however, and didn't know anything to do but repeat the question, emphasizing each syllable of "Row-Anne," which of course made me even less comprehensible than before.

One of the ladies was wearing a black-and-gray-checked coat, and the other was wearing a purple coat. Madame Checked Coat began talking rapidly as she pointed straight ahead. The only word I understood was "gare"—train station. Madame Purple Coat slapped her companion on the arm—they were clearly pals of long standing—and spewed out her opinion as she pointed in the opposite direction. They continued back and forth, pushing and slapping as their voices rose higher, exactly like a well-rehearsed slapstick-comedy act in vaudeville. After several minutes, they somehow came to an agreement, both pointed straight ahead, and repeated "La gare" in unison. Or at least that's what Tracy and I thought they said. As I drove on, we found that we were both thrilled by the encounter, our first ever with actual French people. And the ladies had been sweet and funny and very nice and had tried very hard to help us. What fun it was getting lost in France! If we hadn't been lost, we wouldn't have had this adventure. We decided that most likely we should get off the hill and down into the valley, so we followed any road that descended, and soon enough entered a small town where, miraculously, we saw a train station. Squat and ugly, it looked like a vision of paradise to us. At the first intersection by the train station we saw, clearly marked, a sign pointing toward the road we wanted to Roanne.

There, we stayed in the hotel connected to the restaurant. Our room was larger than the tiny room we'd had in Rome. A heavy curtain with interlocking brown squares covered a large window. A peculiar, abstract print, also mostly brown, hung on one wall. A small television sat on a narrow table. It seemed incongruous to us. Who came to France to watch television? Before dinner, Tracy surprised me by ordering Campari and soda for us both from room service. I had never tasted Campari and had no idea that she liked it. And I didn't understand why she would order it now, since it was Italian, not French. "It's red. I ordered it for the color," she said. "All these browns. The red will brighten up the room."

The waiter set the tray with the drinks on a low white table. Since there weren't any chairs, we sat on the floor beside the table. We kissed and then made a toast to ourselves with our glasses in hand and took a sip. Although I like Campari now, that first sip was unpleasant. Tracy saw my reaction and said, "The second sip will taste better." And it did. I remember the Campari now more distinctly than I remember anything about our spectacular meal at the restaurant.

We were seated side by side on a banquette against a mirrored wall, so we looked across the whole restaurant. The waiter made some suggestions about what dishes we might order and what wine we might drink. We took them all. We were in awe of where we were, both aware that this was a supreme moment in our lives. It was by far the most civilized restaurant we had ever been in. Although it was full, the restaurant was quiet and pleasant and comfortable, even easy-going, not the least stiff. The waiters brought out the orders and served them silently—no serving spoon ever clanked against a plate. And then the waiters silently reappeared at just the right moment to remove plates, silverware, and glasses, again without a sound. We had not known that food or wine could be this

good, or that they could go together so well, or that eating an
evening meal could make us this happy. We pressed our legs
together under the table, and I kissed her hand from time to
time. The next mŏrning, beaming, now more than ever before
filled with expectations for experiences beyond our imagining,
we drove to Paris.

How did we ever find the Hôtel d'Angleterre? We had a
roadmap of France with a small map of Paris on the back. Since
all we had to do was follow major toll roads from Roanne to
Paris, we never got lost on that drive. On the other hand, it was
far from a restful journey. There was no speed limit, so the traffic on the highway resembled a race. Cars swerved from lane
to lane with reckless abandon. No matter how fast I went in the
rented car, someone always caught up with me from behind and
began honking for me to pull over or go faster. I pulled over.

We stopped for gas and lunch at one of the rest stops along
the way. Yes, the drivers were insane, but, once inside and able
to relax for a moment, we marveled at how much cleaner and
nicer the place was, and how much better the food was, than
at similar stops along American turnpikes. (In 2016, during a
drive from the countryside into Paris, I learned that these stops
were no longer so comfortable nor the food so good as they
had been in 1982.) Over coffee and pastry, Tracy and I studied
our apparently adequate map of Paris on the reverse side of our
highway map. Why didn't we realize it was much too small?
Together we decided on a route to the Hôtel d'Angleterre that
looked simple and direct. Tracy felt confident that, while I concentrated on driving, she could navigate to our hotel once we
reached the Périphérique, the huge freeway that circled the outskirts of Paris. From there, the first thing we would do would

be to turn east. We had looked up the word and were proud that we knew that the sign would say "Est."

It was still a ways to April but, yes, shamelessly excited during the weeks before our departure, we would sometimes spontaneously sing "April in Paris," even though neither of us could sing and neither of us knew any of the words except "Chestnuts in blossom / Holiday tables under the treeeeeees." What were "holiday tables"? We didn't know, but Tracy said, "We'll find out when we're there!"

At least we really would be in Paris in April. We could also sing "The last time I saw Paris, her heart was warm and gay." But since we had not yet seen Paris even once, singing that song struck us both as premature.

In Paris in early spring, there are often cloudless days when the sky is so radiantly blue that it casts a glowing aura around the splendors of the city. The day we arrived was such a day, although neither one of us was settled and confident enough to enjoy it. If getting lost in the countryside was a pleasant adventure, getting lost in Paris, at the wheel of a car in the midst of honking traffic, was a frustrating nightmare. By now it was rather late in the afternoon. Rush-hour traffic was just beginning as the road signs on the highway let us know we were approaching the Périphérique. And then, more quickly than we had expected, the Périphérique was looming just ahead of us. There were two signs. Both separately and together, they seemed to be playing an inspired, demonic joke on us. One sign, in addition to a number of unfamiliar French place-names, said "Nord"—north—and the other, in addition to a number of different but also unfamiliar French place-names, said "Ouest"—west. Neither sign said "Est."

I said, "Which way do you think I should go?"

"Uhhhhh . . ." Tracy said as she turned the map back and forth in her hands. How was she supposed to know?

I chose "Ouest," simply because I wouldn't have to change lanes, and the traffic was intimidating. We could see what had to be Paris to our right. I saw an exit for the Avenue de Versailles and took it impulsively: at least I recognized the name. Very quickly, we were off the freeway and on a street in Paris. We had arrived. But where were we? Tracy was turning the map back and forth as we both looked frantically for street names. There weren't any that we could see. Finally, at a stoplight, one of us saw white letters on a small blue plaque on the corner of a building. It said "Avenue de New York." That was a little bit comforting, but, still, where were we? Right Bank or Left Bank? And, either way, how did we get from wherever we were to the Hôtel d'Angleterre at 44 rue Jacob?

We finally figured out that we were on the Right Bank, although I don't remember how. And I no longer have any idea how we managed to get over to the Left Bank and find the rue Jacob. It's a well-known street with more than its share of history, lined then and now with galleries, studios, and specialty shops selling fine fabrics or ceramics. But it's also narrow and somewhat hermetic, being sandwiched between the broad Boulevard Saint-Germain and the river. And it's one-way. Our thrill when we at last turned onto the street changed to anguish when we realized that we were at 60 rue Jacob, not 44, and the numbers got higher as we drove in the only direction we could go. At least we could pull over and figure out how to navigate the one-way streets to circle back to the rue de Seine, from which we could start back down the rue Jacob from its beginning to number 44. There, after an extended struggle with Parisian traffic, we found a small, white, unprepossessing building that was our hotel. We hurriedly hauled our luggage from the car to just inside the door—there was no doorman or porter—and after a quick kiss, I left Tracy with the luggage to check in. Surely, there would be someone to help her. I got back behind the wheel to return the rented car.

There was an address on the rental contract, and now it was my turn to rotate the Paris map back and forth in my hands as I tried to find the street. It turned out to be on the other side of the river. By now it was dark, and the small blue-and-white street signs on the corners of buildings, which had been difficult to see in daylight, were impossible to see from the car. Several times, I pulled over at an intersection and got out to see where I was. But, after much guesswork and frustration, I did at last find the office of the rental-car company, or at least I found *an* office of *a* rental-car company. The address was correct, but the name on the contract and the name on the door did not match. And, of course, since it was early evening, the office was closed. I didn't care. I parked the car on the street and dropped the keys along with a note showing where I had left the car through a slot in the door. I walked away hoping for the best. I never heard anything about a missing car from any rental company, so I guess I was lucky.

Faced now with getting back to the hotel on the other side of the river, I saw a Métro station nearby and boldly went down the steps to try it. I knew the Saint-Germain-des-Prés stop was very close to the rue Jacob. Studying the map in the station, I figured out which direction to take and saw where I would have to transfer to another train. I bought a ticket, plunged into the long tunnel beyond the turnstile, and soon found the platform. In a few moments, a train arrived and I got on. As we passed the next stop, I was relieved to see that I was going in the right direction. I reached the transfer point, got on the other train, and a short while later emerged from the Saint-Germain-des-Prés station. I knew the way from there to the hotel. I was filled with pride and energy. I had done it, I had found my way home in Paris. At the hotel desk, I learned our room number, climbed the stairs, and knocked at the door. Tracy opened the door and stepped back demurely. In a rush, I started telling her about my triumphal adventure on the Métro. Very quickly, but still too late to prevent her from becoming annoyed, I saw that, for our first night in Paris, Tracy had bathed, combed her hair, put on perfume and makeup, and was wearing black lingerie that I had never seen.

·   ·   ·

I groveled that night until I got a slight smile from her, something considerably less than a beaming, radiant smile, but a smile nonetheless, and the next morning we could laugh enough to move beyond the night before. We had a very large room on the second floor, overlooking the rue Jacob. An elaborate crystal chandelier hung from a ceiling beam and cast intricate shadows on the walls. Two very tall casement windows had long white curtains with brown fleurs-de-lys. Each window opened onto a small balcony, where it was pleasant to stand and watch the comings and goings on the street below. There was a double bed, a couch, a desk, and a vanity table for Tracy with a large round mirror. The bath was an expanse of white tile with a large tub and a bidet. Today this room would cost 350 euros or more, but it must not have been particularly expensive when we were there, because we never thought about the cost.

We even had our breakfasts brought in on a tray every morning. The woman who served us put the tray on the desk silently, then bowed, accepted my tip with a whispered "Merci," and shuffled backward out of the room, closing the door behind her.

That first morning, the orange juice looked fresh, and little wisps of steam rose out of both the carafe of coffee and the white pitcher of warm milk. Tracy poured coffee and milk into a cup, took a sip, and then closed her eyes and slowly swallowed. "Heaven," she said. The croissants were in a basket wrapped in a white cloth. They were still warm. She put some butter on one and took a small bite and once again closed her eyes. "Mmmmmm," she said. She tore a piece off, buttered it, and said, "You have to taste this." I opened wide and she put the morsel in my mouth. "Isn't that the best thing you have ever tasted in your life?" she said. In that moment it actually was, even better than the meal we had had at Les Frères Troisgros. I remember the moment Tracy put that warm, buttered croissant into my mouth better than any of the much finer meals we had during that visit, or on other trips we made over the years. We ate slowly, exclaiming over every bite of bread and every sip of coffee. That was our first meal in Paris.

The neighborhood enchanted us. There were the famous cafés—the Deux Magots, the Café de Flore, and, across the street, the Brasserie Lipp. Fine shops lined the Boulevard Saint-Germain. The ancient Church of Saint-Germain-des-Prés, dating from the eleventh century, gave some honor and legitimacy to everything nearby, even to sidewalk stands selling crêpes. In those days, Le Drugstore was directly across the boulevard from the Deux Magots. It actually was a drugstore. Tracy bought her cigarettes there and some shampoo. But it also had a large café, and a club that was always filled with high-school and college students in a frenzy of excitement. Seven years earlier, in 1974, Carlos the Jackal had tossed a grenade from the mezzanine into the crowd below, killing two people and injuring forty. But Le Drugstore remained a destination for the young. It was vibrant and humming, and we liked it precisely because it was not traditional. In 1995, Le Drugstore moved to the Champs-Élysées, and its former location is now an Armani store. The liveliness that corner had in those days has disappeared.

After our breakfast of ambrosia, with our green Michelin guide in hand, Tracy and I walked out into Paris and did everything that tourists do. We got lost in the Louvre. Not knowing or caring where we were, we wandered through immense galleries and climbed endless wide staircases, stopping when we saw a painting or sculpture we recognized from history-of-art classes in college. We stumbled upon the *Mona Lisa* and the *Venus de Milo* and the *Winged Victory* and a haunting self-portrait by Rembrandt. At a small counter outside one of the galleries, we bought a ham-and-cheese sandwich on a baguette and two glasses of wine. We split the sandwich and ate it while sitting outside, at a table on a balcony. When we decided to leave, we couldn't find our way out. We finally asked a guard, and then another, and then another, until, tired but triumphant, we spilled out of the Louvre onto the rue de Rivoli.

At Notre-Dame, a wedding was in progress. The whole wedding party was splendidly dressed, and the bride's shimmering white gown seemed to illuminate the otherwise dark and somber sanctuary. We were approached by a woman who spoke perfect English, although she didn't seem to be British or American. She was ingratiating at first, and pointed out some interesting details in the area where we were standing. But when we moved on, she came, too, talking without a single pause, and we couldn't shake her. Finally, she began asking for money for—she said—a charity. I gave her a few francs just to try to get rid of her, but I refused when she asked for more. She seemed incredulous and finally walked away in a huff.

Strangely, in Notre-Dame one morning in March 2019, a few weeks before the fire in April, I was approached, not by the same woman, but by someone very similar. She spoke perfect English and tried to be ingratiating by talking knowledgeably about the nave. Then she started talking about "a donation" as she motioned toward a spooky, ancient priest standing next to a pillar, wearing a long robe and leaning on a crosier. I suppose it's possible that he was only posing as a priest. He peered at me as he lingered in the shadows. I abruptly moved away from the woman and managed to escape, but the encounter was unnerving and distasteful. It was as if time had stood still from that first visit long ago until now. I soon left the church.

Of course, Tracy and I went to the Eiffel Tower and rode up to the top. We had an expensive dinner at a Michelin-starred restaurant, although I don't remember where. We also ate at Chez Maître Paul, on the rue Monsieur le Prince. Back then you could see Maître Paul cooking with intense concentration in the kitchen while his wife seated the guests and took their orders. Tracy was able to identify the ingredients in his famous sauces and listed them in the diary she kept. Except for that first breakfast, it was the best meal we had. We had lunch one day at the Brasserie Lipp. Across the restaurant from us was a table of obviously wealthy Frenchmen who were there when we arrived and were still there, lingering over coffee and cigarettes, when we left. Even though they paid no attention to us, their confidence and self-possession made us feel like intruders.

In those days, a digest named *Pariscope* appeared each Wednesday. Along with quite literate and informed reviews, it listed every movie, play, gallery opening, lecture, reading, concert, and any other cultural event in Paris that week. It also had a section of several pages devoted to what it called "Spectacles." Spectacles were live sex shows. If we hadn't exactly expected to find such entertainment in Paris, neither were we very surprised when we saw that it was there. Here we were in Paris for the first time, and here we were open to all the city had to offer, soooooooo . . .

Le Théâtre des 2 Boules was on the rue des Écoles in the Latin Quarter, not far from our hotel. Not only was it the spectacle closest by; it had by far the most appealing ad. (I've learned since that the ad was painted by the pinup artist Aslan, whose work now commands respectable prices on the Internet.) We entered the small theater late in the afternoon. There were a few men alone, but also five or six other couples more or less like ourselves. Everything looked perfectly ordinary except that a rope net extended from the top of the stage to the rear of the room. When we sat in seats in the third row, the net was only twenty inches or so above our heads. Tracy and I looked at each other. We could always tell what the other was thinking, but now our thoughts were glaringly obvious: Would they? Could they?

Onstage, a pretty woman in her twenties was performing a vigorous striptease. The music was loud, and the audience sat perfectly still and silent. When she was nude, she came into the audience. One by one, she sprawled across the lap of each man, emitting little cries and flirtatious giggles. She sat on my knees with her back to my chest, took both of Tracy's hands, and used them to caress her breasts. After she had visited each man in the audience, she climbed back up on the stage and bowed as the lights went down.

We were all left sitting in the dark. There was a cough or two, but otherwise the theater was completely silent. After a long pause, the stage lights came back on. A woman was sitting in a chair on one side of the stage, and a man and a woman were sitting on a small couch on the other side, although the stage was so small that they weren't really very far apart. All three performers were young and dressed like bohemian students. The women both had telephones and were talking. We couldn't understand the dialogue, but its overall meaning was clear enough—the woman next to the man was inviting the other woman over to join them. They both hung up, and the lights went down but came back up just a few seconds later. The single woman had joined the pair on the small couch, and the three of them were kissing, caressing, and slowly unbuttoning and unzipping. Then our unspoken questions were answered: yes, they would, and, yes, they could.

The two women lay down on the net first, and then the man joined them. These attractive kids didn't just go through the motions: they seemed to be deriving at least some pleasure from their activities. But the erotic effect for me—and for Tracy as well, as I learned when we talked later—was severely diluted by our apprehension that the net would break loose, and three naked and entwined French students would crash down on our heads. Afterward, at a café with a carafe of wine, we imagined all the breaks, bruises, and black eyes that would have followed the net's breaking. "We would have to tell our kids that we were at a party and it got out of hand," Tracy said.

"They wouldn't buy it."

"Well, maybe not," Tracy said, "but they wouldn't buy the truth, either."

.   .   .

In the afternoons, we had coffee at the Deux Magots, and came back there for brandy after dinner. All along Saint-Germain, the sidewalk tables were crowded. Street performers and musicians came and went, hoping for tips, which they got. One wore a derby, baggy pants, and a huge, painted bow tie made of cardboard. He would pick out someone walking along the boulevard and, following very closely behind, mimic the way his selected victim walked. He was brilliantly inventive and hysterically funny. If the person he was mimicking stopped and turned around, perhaps beginning to wonder why everyone at the tables along the street was laughing, the clown could drop his pose in an instant and appear natural. There was nothing his victim could do but walk away, bewildered. That was even funnier.

We were deliriously happy during the days that followed. Every time we sat down in a restaurant, it was an adventure. Every street we walked down was exciting, unknown territory. Every store we entered contained treasures we could never have imagined. We visited E. Dehillerin, a store that has been selling cooking utensils in Les Halles since 1820. It has plank floors, and ancient wooden shelves stained a dark brown that display an apparently infinite variety of knives, pots, whisks, strainers, and oddly shaped objects whose purpose neither

Tracy nor I could imagine. We stayed for more than an hour, while Tracy practically caressed the pots and bowls and spatulas and all the rest. There was even a mold in the shape of a lamb.

Just across the rue des Rennes from Le Drugstore was a small dress shop run by an impossibly pretty young woman with short blond hair. Tracy was instinctively drawn into the store. As she tried on clothes, I stood near the entrance, listening, without understanding, as the proprietress talked to her "maman" on the phone. These conversations were long and animated. When Tracy emerged from the dressing room, the young proprietress would put down the telephone and adjust the dress Tracy was trying on, nod approvingly, and then pick up the phone and continue talking to maman. We visited several times, but Tracy hesitated to buy anything. Finally, she bought a very light wool coat. It was bright red and had black buttons from the hem up to the neck. The coat was probably a copy of a Givenchy, since it looked like something Audrey Hepburn might have worn in *Charade*. It was perfect for Tracy. She looked so glamorous—une Parisienne!—walking along the Boulevard Saint-Germain in her red coat and round sunglasses with black frames, her wavy black hair radiant in the sunlight. She had found just the right costume for the role she wanted to play, a role that suited both her and me. We held hands as we walked along the boulevard. "Je t'aime," she whispered in my ear.

"Moi aussi," I answered. That was a lame response, but it was the best I could do in French.

Tracy let it pass. "You need a hat," she said. "Let's go buy you a hat."

And we did. It was a dark-blue Kangol driving cap, which

we dubbed my "chapeau." With my hat and her coat and both of us in sunglasses, we felt transformed, walking along the streets of Paris incognito, our real identities hidden. Once, we stopped and looked at our reflection in a store window, and we laughed out loud.

But Tracy hardly wore the coat at all after we returned home, and I never put on my chapeau. What had been so appealing in Paris stuck out rather pretentiously in the shopping centers and neighborhood streets of Austin. The red coat hung in a closet, a pleasant reminder of the personas we had once briefly managed to assume.

CHAPTER THREE

Do You Find Paris Amusing?

Tracy and I were married in September 1975. We were happy with her two young daughters from her first marriage and our daughter and son; we both wanted the life we were living with them. But that was Austin. Paris was Paris.

Tracy knew there would be a difference before I did. That's why she had planned our first night in Paris before we had even arrived. But I saw the difference soon enough, holding her close to me at the top of the Eiffel Tower, or kissing her gently in the intense and unflattering light of Chez Maître Paul. We were enthralled by Paris because we both believed in the romantic mythology about the city. We had read *The Sun Also Rises* and *A Moveable Feast*. We had seen *An American in Paris* and *Gigi*. We had played record albums by Édith Piaf at top volume. We knew the stories of the Paris of Picasso and Modigliani, of Degas and Renoir and Monet. We had read *Père Goriot* and *Cousin Bette* in translation and had dipped into Proust. What we expected from Paris was the summation of everything beautiful and civilized infused with romance. And now here we were in the real Paris, and the real Paris turned out to be even more beautiful than we had thought it would be, more intoxicating, more romantic, and bursting with exciting possibilities that were inconceivable elsewhere. Her coat and my chapeau—we called them our "disguises"—were important and fun, but they were also simply our first tentative steps toward entering the world we saw before us now in Paris.

Tracy's name at birth was Tracy Lynn Lewis. She grew up in Amarillo, which is a somewhat isolated community in the Texas Panhandle, where the endless flat prairie and the big sky both stretch forever in every direction. Paris, crowded and abundant, is very different from all that emptiness. In the Texas Panhandle, the light at sunset, refracted by clouds, takes on multiple shades of red and orange and even purple. Often dramatically beautiful, it seems to touch the ground along the distant horizon. When storms are coming, their dark clouds can be seen far away, long before the storm arrives. When those clouds appear, it's time to take cover. High wind, pelting rain, and deafening thunder can last for hours. The sky and the land force people there in on themselves and make the philosophically inclined among them wonder what significance they might have in the face of such spectacular natural forces. The most famous artist who ever lived in the area was Georgia O'Keeffe, who taught painting at the college in nearby Canyon, Texas. She responded to the landscape by finding lush sensuality in the petals of blooming flowers. She moved on from Amarillo after a while, as many other sensitive artists, known and unknown, have done. For decades, anyone with ambition or mere wanderlust had no trouble getting out of town. The most fabled highway in America, Route 66, ran right through Amarillo and led directly to Los Angeles.

Tracy came from a line of strong and beautiful frontier

women. Her grandmother Sadie Nance Oliver was related to John Nance Garner, the vice president under Franklin Roosevelt from 1932 until 1941. He would be totally forgotten today except for his comment that the vice presidency is "not worth a bucket of warm piss." Sadie's husband, W. T. Oliver, had died years before Tracy and I married, but Sadie was still alive and not yet vague and confused, as she would be in the years before her death in 1992. She had never cut her hair in her life and wore it coiled around her head. I was told that when Sadie's hair hung loose it fell far below her waist. Of course, I never, ever saw it hanging loose. It was simply unthinkable that Sadie would allow such a thing to any man except her husband.

Sadie always referred to her husband as "Mr. Oliver." They lived on a remote, treeless, windswept ranch on the plains outside Amarillo—not that there was much to Amarillo one hundred years ago, when they moved into the ranch house. The Olivers' house was on a slight rise that passed for a hill in that country. There was a barn and pens and a shed or two, but no other house—in fact, no other building of any kind—could be seen in any direction. The house had a Victorian-trimmed porch and green shutters. Inside, it was furnished with heavy, ornate French furniture and Turkish carpets that Sadie had ordered from Europe. When Tracy was a little girl, that imposing furniture was her first connection with France.

Sadie and Mr. Oliver had four children, three girls and a boy. Shirley, the youngest girl, and beautiful herself, was Tracy's mother. Shirley and Tracy both smoked for most of their lives, but neither one ever lit a cigarette in front of Sadie. Toward the end of her life, Sadie was moved to a nursing home, where she refused to allow any male nurses to attend to her.

"Oh, Mother," Shirley said, "those nurses have seen it all. It's just work to them." But Sadie was adamant. "Men never get tired of seeing *that*," she said.

Quentin Lewis, Tracy's father, owned and ran the Lewis Gas Marts—a local chain of filling stations. There was one on Route 66 where it cut through town. Quentin had gone to the University of Oklahoma, which was closer to Amarillo than the University of Texas in Austin, but Tracy didn't want to go to Oklahoma. Instead, she showed up at the University of Texas in 1960, driving a red Austin-Healey Sprite, which remained her favorite car for the rest of her life. She pledged a sorority, majored in history, learned Spanish, was featured in the yearbook as a campus beauty, got married to an ambitious financial-tycoon-to-be, had two girls, lived in a nice house in a tony neighborhood in Dallas, and was miserable. She left her husband twice for short periods, taking the girls with her, first to Taos, New Mexico, and then to Austin, where I saw her that day in the doorway of the bullpen. When she did finally divorce, I found stories to write for the magazine that would take me time and again to Dallas.

Very quickly, we were very much in love, but that may have been why it was an odd courtship. We just skipped over the preliminaries without even mentioning them and began rehearsing what a life together would be. One night, for dinner, we drove to Ponder, Texas, northwest of Dallas, population five hundred or fewer. The only sites of interest there were the Ranchman's Ponder Steakhouse, where we had come to eat, and the building that held the first bank that Bonnie and Clyde had tried to rob. They failed, partly from incompetence but mostly because there was no money in the bank. The Ranchman's Ponder Steakhouse still gets good reviews on the Internet. Our steaks were tough and flavorless, but I understand why there are good reviews. Of course, it's possible that the restaurant has improved since 1975. More likely, as I have learned during a lifetime in Texas, if you drive far out of your way to eat in a particular place, you tend to be grateful for anything even marginally acceptable.

On another summer afternoon, under a relentless sun, we took the two girls to a popular amusement park called Six Flags Over Texas. At the time, they were five and six. They were always very proper and polite around me, even though they were not at all sure how they were supposed to act with me, nor was I sure how to act with them. At the park, we drank soda, ate ice cream, stood in interminable lines to take disappointing rides, and at sundown, six hours later, sank exhausted back into the car.

I set out for the highway back to Dallas, and before long the girls fell asleep in the back. Now it was completely dark. Tracy directed me the wrong way on a freeway interchange, and after twenty minutes or so ours was the only car on a four-lane highway plowing straight ahead into the night. Somehow we discovered our mistake, somehow we made our way back to Tracy's house and put the girls to bed, somehow we kept seeing each other, somehow we got married, and somehow we stayed together for thirty-five years. I believe that our strong connection was created in that first moment we saw each other. Tracy told me later that she had felt something powerful in that moment, too. We eventually learned that the French call it a "coup de foudre," a bolt of lightning.

Although that moment sustained us, it didn't prevent problems. She had a natural gift for communicating with children. Above all with her own, of course, but with any children at all.

If there were parties that included children, Tracy was always down on the floor with the young ones. She talked to them directly as peers, not as children, but also showed them certain parts of the world they were about to enter. Children, including our own, were neither bored nor out of control around her. Instead, they were fascinated. I didn't dislike children, but I was never drawn to them as she was. It was a great disappointment to her that I didn't immediately closely connect with her two young daughters. It was my fault. I didn't know how to do it.

We rented a large house on Shoal Creek in Austin that was tucked back in a corner between two busy streets. Tracy arrived with the two girls in a fancy Mercedes sedan, which made me uncomfortable. Her father had left the filling-station business and was now running an Allied Van Lines office in Amarillo. He sent a truck to move Tracy's furniture from Dallas to our house in Austin. The movers were two fat, congenial, but very dim bulbs who said during the move that they were going to sleep in the van that night. They seemed astonished that both Tracy and I owned books. When I mentioned that to Quentin, he said, "You don't run across many Harvard graduates in the moving business."

After the two congenial fellows had unloaded the truck, Tracy arranged her furniture. The result was magical. What had been a ragged, counterculture hangout became a very comfortable, attractive, interesting home where the girls had their own bedroom and bathroom and Tracy and I had ours, and there was a living room, a dining room, and a kitchen, completely furnished. One night, when all four of us were in the kitchen, we heard scratching at the door that led to the driveway. It was up to me to answer the door. I opened it cautiously to find a mother raccoon and four small babies lined up behind her, looking wistfully at me. I had two orange tabby cats back then—Buddy and Night Train. I had been wondering why their bowl of cat food just outside the door was always empty.

The two girls enrolled in a good school. We knew people at the magazine, and there were many people Tracy had known during her college days who still lived in Austin, so we had a wide circle of friends. The magazine was prospering enough to have moved from the walk-up offices neighboring the dental laboratory into a new high-rise downtown, although it was still close enough that occasionally I walked there. Tracy continued to spend some time doing publicity for the magazine. One afternoon, she announced to the publisher that she had to leave right away. "My girls just told me that they didn't believe in wishes," she said, and rushed off to fulfill a wish or two for them. This incident became part of the lore of the early days at the magazine.

The house was across a broad avenue from a park with a basketball court where, late in the afternoon, I would often go to enter pickup games. It's possible, even probable, that when you are that young—Tracy was thirty-three and I was thirty-one—you don't really recognize happiness. Or if you do recognize it, you are not really sure it will last. Early in a marriage, each day is both an improvisation, with each of you trying to see what works and what doesn't, and a rehearsal for the roles you will fill in the months and years to come. I see now that both Tracy and I were very happy. When we had disagreements, we managed to work them out. I remember Tracy's joy in coming to embrace me as she or I or both of us made apologies. I was always more than ready to apologize. Tracy had gambled with both her life and the lives of her two girls by marrying me. All that I had had to offer was love for her and my desire to be a husband and a father. I feared failing at either role. When I saw her become angry, my stomach would sink to the floor.

After a month or two, I did a semi-heroic thing in that house on Shoal Creek. One day, it started to stink. There was no escaping the stench. Where was it coming from? What was there to do? I walked around the perimeter of the house several times before I found a small grate that led to a crawl space under the floor. I managed to squeeze through. The space between the dirt and the floor of the house was very narrow. There wasn't room to get on my hands and knees to crawl, so I had to sort of swim along the ground on my stomach. With a flashlight, I eventually found the rotting corpse of a cat—it must have somehow gotten in and then, unable to find its way out, starved to death. I grabbed its tail, dragged it outside, and threw it into the trash. The stench in the house disappeared. Tracy and the girls were visibly relieved and grateful. Odd as it may seem, dragging off that dead cat was the first time I felt deeply what it means to be a husband and a father in a household.

.   .   .

I grew up in Kansas City, Missouri. Ernest Hemingway had lived there from October 1917 until April 1918, while working for *The Kansas City Star*. He was eighteen. I knew this when I was fairly young, and it fascinated me. I believe that my mother, Vivian, who liked Hemingway, must have told me. I learned as well, either from her or from my own reading, that he lived in Paris after leaving Kansas City. And I ran across this brief moment in *The Sun Also Rises*. Jake Barnes, the narrator of the novel, has arrived at a bal musette with a prostitute he had picked up at a restaurant earlier in the evening. Someone has brought a young novelist over to meet him. The young novelist speaks first:

> *"You're from Kansas City, they tell me," he said.*
> *"Yes."*
> *"Do you find Paris amusing?"*
> *"Yes."*
> *"Really?"*

This brief exchange exasperates Jake, who becomes very angry. I think I knew even in high school that there was much of importance about Paris and Kansas City and other things, including sex, that are present but unsaid in that brief dialogue.

Since I knew that it was possible to have lived in Kansas City and then to live in Paris, I felt a link between the two cities. As I was growing up, I even thought that the two cities could be quite similar. This thought was less fanciful than it might seem, just as long as the comparison is not pushed too hard. In those days, Kansas City prided itself on having, at least to a degree, the gracefulness of European cities. The brick-and-granite buildings downtown, not far from the banks of the sluggish Missouri River, were unmistakably part of a Midwestern American city. But not far from them, to the south, where blocks of houses began, there were broad boulevards lined with trees, grassy parks, great fountains, flowery esplanades, and an impressive art museum on the top of a hill. Like Paris, Kansas City is a river town, and, also like Paris, it had once been a center of art, although that art in Kansas City was jazz. In fact, between the two world wars, years when the corrupt Pendergast regime ran the city and the nightlife was wild and wide

open, Kansas City promoted itself as the "Paris of the Plains."
Ladies there bought their nicest dresses at Harzfeld's Parisian, and a leading hotel offered a Parisian Surprise Luncheon.
The vaudeville theater was likened to the Paris Opera House,
although by my day it had become the Follies Burlesque. And
then there was the looming television-broadcast tower just off
Main Street, right in the center of town and impossible not to
see, especially at night when it was lit red. The television station called it "the Eye-Full Tower," to the great embarrassment
and disgust of my mother.

Although extremely subtle, funny, and intelligent, she was
also acutely aware and embarrassed that she had never gone
to college, that her formal education went no further than
a diploma from the high school in De Witt, Missouri. That
made her sensitive to any social or intellectual slight. Once, a
woman she had just met said, "We are old Kansas City. What
are you?" My mother fumed about that for years afterward. She
did not think that she was a country rube, or that her family
were rubes, or that the people she knew in Kansas City were
rubes. And she didn't need to make any apologies for not having attended college, although she didn't need to mention it,
either. And now here was this inescapable, ugly tower with a
name that she thought, correctly, sounded so hick. It grated
on her, even though—or, rather, especially because—she was
never able to go to Paris, or anywhere in Europe, or even New
York until she was well into her fifties.

My natural father was killed in the Pacific during World
War II. It's curious to me that in different places throughout my
life—in high school, in graduate school, at work in Austin—
I have made close friends who I later learned had lost their

fathers, as I had, when they were young children. That invisible absence is somehow a bond among us.

I wasn't yet three when my mother remarried. My stepfather, William Curtis, treated me splendidly always, though he was perhaps a little remote from me and his own three children. His mind was usually elsewhere. He was eager to get to his law office in the morning, and worked at home after dinner every night except Saturday, when he liked to watch *Perry Mason* on television. "Obviously inadmissible," he would often call out when Perry was questioning a witness.

Bill Curtis actually knew a little French from a course in college. His French textbooks were moldering in our basement, along with his books and notes from Harvard Law School. Sometimes I leafed through them, and I found the legal textbooks every bit as impenetrable as the French textbooks. He read serious novels only if they were about World War II, during which he had served in the army in the Pacific. There were copies of *From Here to Eternity*, *The Young Lions*, and *The Naked and the Dead* on our bookshelves. Otherwise, his taste inclined toward Erle Stanley Gardner. But I was surprised one year, during summer vacation, to see him reading *The Girl with the Golden Eyes* by someone named Balzac. When I asked about the book, it turned out that he loved saying that name. He pronounced it "Bal*zac!*" as in "Bal*zac!* Who was Bal*zac!*? We had to read Bal*zac!* in college."

Maybe he liked a certain kind of French novel more than we ever suspected. For some reason, there was a translation of *Mademoiselle de Maupin* by Théophile Gautier on one of our bookshelves. Perhaps it had been a pony during one of his French courses. I thumbed through it one afternoon and returned to it in private many times after that. Its racy story, and the frequent lines of colons in that edition, attracted my adolescent imagination. I assumed that the colons indicated that something had been censored. What were these French men and women doing that was so unspeakably shameful that it had to be hidden? In the 1950s, to say that something was French was also to imply that it was a little saucy. In the early days of television, cancan dances appeared at the slightest excuse. The common assumption was that Paris was the place where forbidden things were not only allowed but encouraged, a city where nudity and sex were everywhere all the time. In my mind, that copy of *Mademoiselle de Maupin*, which I presumed had been redacted, was vivid proof that this libertine image of Paris was true. (Imagine my disappointment years later when, reading portions of *Mademoiselle de Maupin* in French, I realized that the colons had been put there by Gautier himself.)

Then, in 1957, when I was thirteen and very impressionable, the final, incontrovertible proof of Parisian licentiousness arrived in Kansas City. *And God Created Woman* appeared at a movie theater on Grand Avenue. It starred a new young sexpot named Brigitte Bardot. That the movie had been allowed into the United States at all, although in a severely edited version, had been national news that reached even me and my excitable contemporaries, who seldom read the papers except for the sports page. We couldn't see the film: the theater was not going to admit anyone under eighteen. Besides, we were also too young to drive, and asking our parents to take us to that movie was unthinkable. But our imaginations soared as we whispered among ourselves about what the film might contain.

Any photograph of Brigitte Bardot electrified us. The other sex symbols of the era—Marilyn Monroe, for example—

seemed to be from a different, older generation and lived in a different, older world that didn't include us and that we didn't aspire to anyway. Brigitte Bardot, although she was only eight years younger than Monroe, was entirely new and different and, of course, French. One afternoon a year or two later, I saw a review of another of her movies in *Time* magazine that included a picture of her wrapped in a white towel, standing by a bathtub. Her abundant hair hung over her shoulders and all the way down her back, and her lovely legs were bare beneath the bottom edge of the towel. This was the first time it occurred to me that I might someday want to embrace Paris.

As I look back now, I think it's possible that this photograph never existed at all, that it is a chimera that I have summoned up across many years of idle imaginings. I haven't seen the photograph since that afternoon, and in a search of the Internet I discovered some similar images but not that one. Still, my memory of seeing it is so vivid—I even remember where I was in our house when I was reading the magazine—that I can't help believing the photograph really must exist.

· · ·

Before our first visit to Paris, Tracy had read in a guidebook about the Château de Chantilly, which is about thirty miles north of Paris, just outside the small town of the same name. Its museum contains one of the greatest collections of Old Master art in France, perhaps the greatest after the Louvre. Its library is equally important, for its immense number of rare books and manuscripts, some of which date as far back as the tenth century.

We took a train to Chantilly and asked for directions to the château at a tabac. The man pointed down the street and said the château was straight ahead. Could we walk there? Oh yes, of course. So off we went, and walked for what seemed quite a long time before we came to the grandstands of a racetrack. From there we could see the château far in the distance, across a large pasture. It seemed odd that there wasn't a road or even a path that led to an entrance to the château, but we started walking all the same.

It turned out to be heavy going. The pasture was a little muddy, and the grass was long so we had to lift our feet high and take exaggerated steps. But we kept on. Our excitement rose with each clumsy step, because the closer we got the more beautiful the château appeared to us. Perhaps it was a little bulky, but it had high windows and a graceful roofline. Again, it seemed odd that there was no suitable entrance, although we could see a small, unmarked door. When we finally reached the door, we didn't know what to do. Should we just open it and walk in? That didn't seem right, so Tracy knocked lightly. We waited, but there was no response. I knocked quite a bit louder than she had, but still no one answered. I tried the door, and to our surprise it opened easily. As we walked through, we both started laughing. We were rubes after all. We were in the stables.

We went back outside, skirted around the stables, and found the real château. It had, after all, a very elaborate entrance, with a tranquil pond, a stone bridge across a moat, multiple arches, and two niches on either side of the gate that held replicas of Michelangelo's *Slaves*. The originals, which are now in the Louvre, had once stood there.

Inside, we found the long gallery where the famous collection of paintings was displayed. They hung closely side by side, the way museums displayed paintings centuries ago. The paintings were immensely impressive, but we couldn't study them as we would have liked. They were much more than we could really absorb in a short visit, and now, thanks to our diversion into the stables, we were running out of time and needed to rush to the station so as not to miss the train back to Paris.

We talked solemnly to each other as we sat on the train. So far, our trip had been a series of wonderful, almost magical experiences, from seeing the Sistine Chapel to our meeting the two French ladies at the side of the road and then taking that first bite of croissant in our hotel room. We had expected Chantilly to be another of these wondrous experiences, and it was, to a degree. But to a greater degree it had been grand, distant, and impenetrable. We had just been made to see that, to understand this place, even genuinely to experience this place, was going to require much more from us than just showing up here and there and casting quick glances. Our expectations, grand as they were, seemed off the mark. They didn't really harmonize with all that we were seeing. There was more around us here, in France and in Paris especially, than we were really prepared to understand. We didn't want to turn the pleasure of new places and new experiences into work, or to remove chance and serendipity from our days abroad. But we now realized that some more preparation and considerably less hurry would reveal a different, deeper world to us, a world that, before this trip, we had had no way of knowing was there.

However, nothing we had seen before was lost. Everything had counted and made us ready for and open to this revelation. All during our visit, we were much in awe of the civilization that we found in the many monuments all around us. We found the churches especially imposing. Inside them, we spoke to each other in whispers even if no one else was nearby. We walked slowly around the periphery, pausing in front of every chapel to admire the mural or the sculpture or the stained-glass windows. A time or two, we had had the luck to enter a church when the organist was practicing. We would sit together in the sanctuary, as Paris bustled all around us outside, and listen.

I had stopped going to church the moment I left home for college. I remember being stunned, during my first weeks away at Rice University when I saw some classmates get up on Sunday morning, put on coats and ties, and go off to church. Why would anyone do that if his parents didn't make him? Although we seldom went to church together, Tracy was a believer, and was even for several years on the altar guild of the Episcopal church where her funeral service was eventually held. But the religion we saw in the cathedrals of Paris, in their darkness as well as in the light through their stained-glass windows, in their great height and weight as well as in the delicate paintings in their chapels, and in their countless representations of the Virgin, the crucifixion, and multitudes of saints and martyrs— all that seemed more profound and far more *religious* than anything offered in Episcopal churches in Austin or Amarillo or at the synthetic mega-churches that we saw in Houston and Dallas. Some of those differences weren't specific to France but were simply the differences between a Catholic church no matter where and a Protestant church no matter where, but not all of them. There was real power in the size of the churches and in their heavy stone walls, real mystery in their darkness and depth and hidden corners. And there was real glory in their tall windows and gesturing statues and heavy golden crucifixes. It was all appealing, although we found that it could also be repelling in equal measures. Why was the Church so rich? Why was it so hierarchical, with Tracy and me and everyone else at the bottom? Were these relics of saints the real thing? Was that really, really Jesus's crown of thorns in Notre-Dame? You could see why the Revolution opposed both the monarchy and the Church.

Tracy would be intrigued and probably a little amused to know that, from time to time when I'm in Paris, I go to a mass at eleven on Sunday morning. I've read in newspapers both in Paris and at home that these days the churches in France are empty, but in my experience that's not true. If I arrive for mass at ten-forty-five, there will be only a few people sitting in the rows of chairs in the sanctuary. I usually take a chair near the front. When the service begins, I turn to look behind me, and invariably plenty of people have slipped in and almost all the seats are taken. At one point during the service, the priest asks the congregation to greet their neighbors. In doing so, you shake hands with everyone in reach. I love this moment. When else am I going to reach out and speak to an elderly widow, an African gentleman whose gray trousers have a knife crease, or a young couple standing arm in arm? I like to go to Saint-Germain-des-Prés, near the Deux Magots and the Café de Flore. It's the oldest church in Paris and rather small, but the congregation is filled with young families. I also like Saint-Eustache, by Les Halles, where they celebrate a very high mass, with as many as seven priests officiating. There is incense and reverberating music from the largest organ in France and a priest uses an aspergillum to sprinkle the congregation with holy water. Saint-Eustache is one of the larger churches in Paris; the transept is so high that it almost seems to fade into a distant sky, which had to be the intended effect.

After the mass, I make the short walk from Saint-Eustache to Au Pied de Cochon, the restaurant I adore above all others in

Paris. I choose their onion soup, which is the best there is anywhere in the world, and a nicely priced carafe of white wine. Au
Pied de Cochon is a pretty restaurant that has been open since
1947, and it's one restaurant where I don't mind sitting alone, at
a table with shining silverware on a crisp, spotless white table-
cloth. E. Dehillerin, the store with cooking supplies, is also
nearby, and reminds me of the long visit there that Tracy and I
made together during our first trip to Paris.

After I've ordered, while I'm waiting for my onion soup,
with the carafe of wine in front of me, I can reflect, and do
reflect, on why I especially miss Tracy during the masses I
attend. I miss her then because that is precisely when my most
intimate feelings tell me that she is with me, even though Tracy
and I never attended a mass together. We did wander through
Saint-Germain-des-Prés on our first visit to Paris, since it was
close to the Hôtel d'Angleterre, but we never went to Saint-
Eustache. Besides, even if we had gone to a mass together,
it was the Episcopal Church she believed in, not the Roman
Catholic one. I didn't then and don't now believe in either
church. But there is something holy that I find in the great mass
of Saint-Eustache and the other grand Parisian cathedrals, and
that something is emptiness. I don't mean nothing. I mean an
emptiness, an emptiness that is there and palpable, an emptiness that is nevertheless something and that contains invisible
multitudes, an emptiness that is sanctified by the mass. I believe
that Tracy must be somewhere in that emptiness. The bigger
the church, the bigger the emptiness it contains, and the more
likely it is that she is there.

CHAPTER FOUR

Her Bilingual Husband

When we left Paris after our first visit in 1982—Tracy returned to Austin; I went on to Germany—we did not know that it would be twelve years before we saw Paris again. The offer from Germany of a plane ticket and a tour, something completely unexpected that was too good to pass up, had given us permission to go to Europe the first time, and spend money and leave the children behind in the care of their grandparents Quentin and Shirley. Without any such permission, taking an expensive trip to Europe just because we wanted to seemed like a selfish extravagance. Instead, for several summers in a row, we drove to Colorado with the children. We had a luggage rack on the roof of our car filled with fishing rods, swimming suits, golf clubs, and hiking boots. We did continue trying to learn French, in a classroom, with instructional tapes, or with a tutor. We read Balzac. He's usually quite specific about where his characters live and what routes they take when moving around Paris. It was fun to find these streets in the blue Michelin Paris map we had bought, especially if they turned out to be near places we had happened on ourselves. But that was as close to

Paris as we got until 1994, when by chance we got permission
to go again.

One evening early in the year, someone at the stables where
I rode horses gave me a brochure from a company that booked
rides on horseback in many European countries as well as in
South America, Africa, and even Mongolia. This outfitter had
a wide selection of rides in France.

My connection with horses began when our young-
est daughter, Vivian, had the typical girlish infatuation with
horses. Tracy and I began driving her to stables once a week
after school and on Saturday mornings. Horses, stables, tack
rooms, riding boots, and riders all existed in a world that was
alien to me. At first I found it frivolous and off-putting. But,
soon enough, I began to recognize the skill involved in horse-
manship and could see the difference between a real rider and
someone who could merely stay on a horse. Sometime around
1990, I started taking lessons myself, and kept on with them for
the next twelve years. After a few years, I passed from being a
merely adequate rider to being perhaps slightly more than adequate, but I had started too late in life to become really good.
Eventually, though, I was able to hold my own in a class twice
a week among the better riders at the stables, most of whom
were women.

The most appealing ride in the brochure, both to Tracy and
to me, was going to be that June. It traversed the Loire Valley,
visiting châteaux along the way. But the ride was expensive,
and became more expensive still when airfare and an irresistible
few days in Paris were added in. We had two children in college
and two teenagers still at home. Normally, this trip would be
such an extravagance that we would feel guilty all the while we
were in France. But I persuaded *Travel Holiday* to let me write a

story for them about the ride. The magazine would take care of
the expenses and pay me a fee besides. Only one complication
remained—Tracy didn't ride. I can still clearly see her face,
white with fear, as she bounced on the back of a trotting horse
the one time she did climb into a saddle. At first, we thought that
Tracy would drive a rented car and rejoin the other riders and
me in the evenings when we stopped at a hotel. But, luckily, the
outfitter of the ride—Paul Bontemps, an appropriate name—
had made efforts to accommodate an elderly German woman
who had always loved horses but couldn't ride anymore. She
would follow the riders in a gig that Paul's son Benjamin, who
was seventeen, would drive. That provided the happy solution:
Tracy could ride with them.

We arrived in Paris on a Friday morning in late June. In the
intervening twelve years, the prices at the Hôtel d'Angleterre
must have risen, or we were simply more conscious of our
budget, or, most likely, both. We stayed just a block or so
east on the rue Jacob, at the Hôtel des Marronniers (chestnut
trees). The doors from the street to the hotel opened onto a
deep, narrow courtyard lined with abundant ferns planted in
long boxes. Inside, a curving staircase by the reception desk
climbed up to our room. It had floral wallpaper and was pleasant enough; what's more, here we were back in Paris. But we
were both too tired from our overnight flight to do much to
celebrate our return. While Tracy took a long bath in the surprisingly spacious marble bathroom, I lay on the bed, looking
through the window at a warren of Parisian rooftops beneath a
blue sky. There were shuttered mansard windows with peeling
paint, small round chimneys, and ancient, spindly television
antennas. Somewhere— I looked but it was impossible to see
where—a large choir was rehearsing. "My sweet Lord," they

sang. "Hallelujah. My sweet Lord . . ." The choir was filled
with rich, swelling voices. Their singing floated invisibly over
the rooftops. Tracy came out of the bathroom wearing a silk
robe. She sat next to me on the bed and brushed out her hair as
we listened to the choir for several minutes without speaking,
lost in our thoughts. But when Tracy did speak, it became clear
that our thoughts were much the same. In a low voice, almost a
whisper, she said, "This is Paris after all, isn't it."

"Yes, this is Paris after all," I said as I took her hand.

.   .   .

The next afternoon, a Saturday, after a brunch of mush-
room omelettes and smoked salmon at the Café de Flore, only
a short walk away, we went to the Gare d'Austerlitz and took a
train an hour south to Orléans, where we met Paul Bontemps,
his son Benjamin, and the other riders at a hotel. There were
eleven of them, all German, Swiss, or Austrian except for one
American woman from Colorado who had given herself this
trip for her fortieth birthday. At dinner, Tracy and I tried our
French, but we dropped it soon enough, since most of the other
riders spoke English well, and young Benjamin spoke halting, schoolboy English. Paul didn't speak a word. Someone
or another would translate his instructions for us. They were a
good-looking group, all about our age, fit, and happily antici-
pating the five days of riding together.

Such rides are called "randonnées," and they're a popular
way to spend a holiday in France. There are randonnées à pied
(on foot), à vélo (by bicycle), à ski, and à cheval (on horseback).
Typically, the group gathers on Saturday evening at an inn in
a village in the countryside. They set out the next morning

behind a leader. Meanwhile, an assistant loads all the luggage in a van and drives to set up a picnic lunch at a place along the way. After lunch, the ride proceeds, and the assistant cleans up the lunch and drives on to the hotel where everyone will spend the night.

That morning, we all rode in the van out to the farm where the horses had been stabled for the night. My mount was named Ulette. She was a powerfully built bay with four spotted socks and a long body. She was so tall that when I stood beside her to saddle up, I could barely see over her withers. She seemed entirely unconcerned as I buckled on the saddle and a pair of saddlebags Paul had given me.

The gig turned out to be little more than a thick plank on two wheels. Barbara, the German woman who would ride with Tracy in the gig, was well into her seventies. She had been an English teacher all her life before retiring. She was sunny and smiling. Every now and then she would drop in some unexpected English expression such as "See you later, alligator." Tracy liked Barbara immediately when they met at dinner.

The sky was gray and overcast when we all mounted up Sunday morning and started out in one direction behind Paul. The gig, with Benjamin sitting in the middle, between Barbara and Tracy, set off in the opposite direction. We walked for a while along the edge of cultivated fields and then entered a forest. Paul rose in his saddle and turned to look at us. Then he raised his hand and kicked his horse. We all took off at a gallop out of the forest and across open country, a new experience for me. I balanced in my stirrups, told myself to look forward and not down, and tried to keep my heart from rising into my throat. You can feel a horse shifting into high gear when it begins to gallop. The body seems to lengthen, and the ride is actually smoother than at any other gait once the rider learns to relax. I did learn, but it took me a while.

When we stopped for lunch, I was ready to get off Ulette and try to pull myself together, although she had been nothing but easy and obedient. I was really in a mild daze, which felt worse because Tracy and the gig had not yet arrived. Paul seemed unconcerned as we all began bringing buckets full of water from a canal for the horses. Then I thought I heard singing in the distance—"Home, home on the range, / Where the deer and the antelope play." In a few moments, the gig appeared, coming out at the edge of a forest. They were late because they had gotten lost. They had decided to pass the time by singing songs from their native lands, and it was Tracy's turn as they came up to join us.

Tracy had enjoyed the morning, even though riding along in the gig could become boring, and she continued to enjoy the ride during the rest of the week. My afternoon was much better than my morning. I was more confident at a gallop and could enjoy racing across open country or along the edge of a wheat field. I had brought a water bottle to carry with me. By the third day, I was having wine with lunch and putting some in the water bottle, too. One day at lunch Paul said we were going to spend the night at a different hotel from the one his groups usually stayed in. In the middle of the afternoon, as we emerged from a forest, Paul turned to the right. Ulette wanted to turn left. Only when I insisted did she reluctantly go to the right. I learned later that the hotel Paul usually stayed in was to the left. After several days of riding across many miles of countryside, Ulette knew exactly where she was.

Paul was well aware that I was there to write an article. He

always gave Tracy and me the best rooms at the hotels where we
stopped for the night, and, for that matter, I think Ulette might
well have been the best mount in his herd. Usually, we stayed
at three- or four-star country inns; one night, we stopped at a
château with a moat and a drawbridge. Since it doesn't get dark
in the summer in France until ten or so, dinner was always late.
Tracy and I spent the late afternoon and the evening luxuriat-
ing in our fancy room. We took long baths and spent our time
together well and then dressed up a little for dinner. The food
was always local specialties made with meats and produce from
the area. The wine was from the region, too. We were always
relaxed and happy, satiated even, when we slipped into bed near
midnight.

After five idyllic days of riding and dining together, we
were a happy but also somewhat melancholy band on Friday,
our last evening at a hotel, in Tours. The next morning, Tracy
and I took a train to Paris, where we had reserved a room
for three nights at the Hôtel des Deux-Iles, on the Île Saint-
Louis. Tracy had thought that staying on the island would be a
quiet, romantic experience, away from the bustle of the rest of
Paris, allowing us to relax contentedly after the ride. Unfortunately, swarms of revelers clogged the streets around the hotel
at night, and their whoops and general din intruded mightily on
our little love nest.

But, by a happy accident, my mother and two sisters were
going to be in Paris at the same time. When we arrived, they
were about to embark on a tour of Normandy. They were staying at the Hôtel Scribe, on the Right Bank, across a broad
avenue from the Opera. Tracy and I visited them there the
first afternoon we were back in Paris. Once the Germans were
driven from Paris toward the end of World War II, the Scribe

became the gathering place for journalists and photographers covering the war. There's a famous illustration painted by Floyd Davis of Ernest Hemingway, Janet Flanner, Robert Capa, A. J. Liebling, and many others, all drinking at the bar in the Scribe. The Scribe turned out still to be a rather grand place; the imposing lobby had black-and-white marble floors, tall marble vases, and marble side tables all around, and a peaked glass ceiling high above. My sisters were sharing a room, so we met in my mother's room, which had a separate bedroom and a large sitting area with a couch and several stuffed chairs.

My family all adored Tracy, and she was always at the height of her charm when she was with them. She talked about singing cowboy songs as she rode on the gig through the countryside with her two companions: "And then Barbara sang German songs and Benjamin sang French songs and we would take turns driving." My mother asked her if it was hard to drive the gig. "No, no, not at all. To go right you pull on the right rein. To go left, you pull on the left. To go straight, which is ninety percent of the time, you don't do anything. You just think of another cowboy song to sing."

Tracy and I had brought a good bottle of red wine with us, which we all decided to drink right then. But there were no wineglasses. I called down to room service. Showing off, I spoke in French to the man who answered. "Bonjour, monsieur. Pourriez-vous apporter cinq tasses à la chambre 2077?"

"Cinq tasses, monsieur?"

"Oui."

He hesitated before saying, "D'accord, monsieur."

In a few moments there was a knock at the door, which I opened in a grand gesture. There stood a confused waiter balancing a round tray with five coffee cups. Oh yes, I remembered too late—"une tasse" means a cup; a glass is "un verre."

My mother loved to laugh and was a good storyteller when she was in the mood and had the right audience. I could see that this embarrassing little scene was going right into her repertoire. Her face was red from laughter, and my sisters and Tracy were also laughing. Fortunately for me, the waiter thought it was funny, too, and said he would gladly return with five wineglasses. He did, and I gave him the generous tip that he deserved. I poured the wine. Tracy held up her glass. "To my bilingual husband," she said.

CHAPTER FIVE

Dancing to the Mamou Playboys

The following year, 1995, we took our two children to Paris. In fact, we did more than that. Tracy and I planned to spend all of June in France with Vivian and Ben. Vivian and I would go on a horseback ride for a week; then we would meet Ben and Tracy in Lyon, and all four of us would go to an intensive language and cooking school in the country for two weeks. After that, we would spend a week in an apartment in Paris that we had rented. Tracy and I were convinced that all four of us would be speaking French fluently after a month in France and our two weeks of intensive study.

This trip was an irrational extravagance. Not only would I miss work, I would be far away and out of touch with my office for four weeks. That meant I would miss both sending one issue of the magazine to the printer and getting the next issue under way. I did as much advance planning as I could, but I knew that there was no substitute for being in the office, especially if problems arose. No one on the staff said anything to me; they didn't have to. I knew that being gone that long was just on the edge of being irresponsible. And, also irresponsibly, I had to borrow money from my 401(k) account to pay for it all, which I knew was a poor financial decision. Tracy also knew that taking the trip was a foolish indulgence, but we kept quietly planning. We whispered between ourselves like conspirators preparing to confront authority. We both wanted to take the trip, no matter what.

I found a ride for Vivian and me to take in the Dordogne, and in an attempt to justify what we were going to do anyway, I persuaded *The New York Times'* Travel Section to let me write an article about our ride. Vivian and I said goodbye to Tracy and Ben and flew to Paris. After the plane landed, I realized that I was supposed to know what I was doing there. We took a bus into Paris from the airport, and then the Métro from the bus stop to our hotel. On the way to the Métro station, I cashed a two-hundred-dollar traveler's check and carelessly put the wad of bills in my front pants pocket.

I think the combination of jet lag and the need to look assured in front of Vivian didn't leave me at my best. Somehow, I got the wrong tickets or went to the wrong entrance to the Métro or something. At any rate, the turnstile at the entrance refused our tickets and wouldn't turn. Stymied, Vivian and I tossed our bags over the turnstile and then climbed over it ourselves. We got away with it—no one arrived to question us. We lugged our bags down the steps to the train. It arrived quickly, and we got on. Vivian sat down, but I stood by our bags. I was vaguely aware of a man standing rather close to me, but I didn't want to miss our stop and was looking for it, so I didn't pay too much attention to him. We got off at the proper station and climbed out of the Métro. On the way to our hotel, I decided to stop for coffee and a croissant, a rough approximation for Vivian of that first breakfast in Paris that Tracy and I had shared. Although I didn't think this breakfast in the res-

taurant was as transcendent an experience for Vivian as it had
been for Tracy and me, she did like it. That was a small victory,
though. She was sixteen and not easily pleased. When the bill
came, I reached into my front pants pocket for my money. It
wasn't there, not even a single bill. The man in the Métro had
picked my pocket on the train. I glumly cashed another check.
The cost of our month in France had just gone up by two hundred dollars. The following day, we did get to the proper train
station for our trip south. We managed to catch the right train,
and arrived on time in Bergerac, at the rendezvous for the ride.

On the ride to Bergerac, I'd mulled over the experience of
getting robbed. I wasn't happy about the theft, but it had less
effect on me than I would have thought. I was to blame; I had
been heedless and stupid. The man might have been prowling
near the currency exchange, hoping to find an easy prey like me.
More likely, he was watching in the Métro, where I think I must
have pulled out my wad of francs while paying for our tickets.
Then he followed Vivian and me onto the train. He sidled next
to me, did what he did, and got off at the next stop, the richer
by two hundred dollars' worth of francs. At least he hadn't gotten my wallet, with my driver's license and credit cards, or my
passport, all of which would have created horrible bureaucratic
nightmares to cancel and replace. Even as I resolved to be more
careful in the future, as I have been, I had a slight admiration
for the smoothness with which he practiced his métier.

For at least two centuries, every travel guide to Paris has
warned against pickpockets. Robert Bresson's masterpiece
Pickpocket from 1959 is one of several iconic films from that era
about Paris. In museums, in the Métro, and in many tourist des-
tinations, it's common to hear warnings about pickpockets in
several languages over the public address system. Usually, the

warnings are given when the authorities spot gangs of teenaged girls. I learned this one afternoon at the Louvre, when a guard who had gotten on an elevator with Tracy and me wouldn't let a group of three or four girls on with us. She not only blocked the door but forcibly shoved one of the girls away. When the guard saw that I was astonished, she shook her head with her mouth turned down and an air of disgust. "They will rob you," she said in English.

Tracy and I had seen a gang of eight to ten such girls on the train to Chantilly in 1982. They roamed from car to car, shrieking and laughing and generally creating a disturbance. We didn't understand what they were at the time, but we knew instinctively to be wary. Not long after that, as we got on a Métro train at the La Motte–Picquet station in Paris, a girl's hand reached through the closing doors behind us and into Tracy's purse. I saw what was happening and grabbed the girl's wrist. The train's doors closed on her arm, bounced back open, and then closed and opened again, causing alarms to ring and horns to honk insistently. Two elderly Frenchwomen beat on the girl's arm with their fists until she opened her hand, letting Tracy's wallet fall back into her purse, and I let go of the girl's wrist. She snatched back her arm, the sliding doors closed, the train started moving, and one of the Frenchwomen hissed, "Répugnante. Répugnante." And just this May, in 2019, I saw a gang of girls working the crowd in front of the Musée d'Orsay. One had a clipboard holding papers she was asking people to sign, to petition to help "the orphans," while her accomplices lurked nearby, hoping some mark would be distracted while signing the papers on the clipboard.

But these girls are far from the only pickpockets working in Paris. Since being robbed that day in the Métro with Vivian,

I've been careful, especially in crowds. On April 16, the morning after the fire in Notre-Dame, I walked down Boulevard Saint-Michel to see the cathedral. I carefully stashed my wallet in the left front pocket of my jeans and kept my left thumb hooked over the wallet. The crowd that had assembled along the south bank of the Seine to see the cathedral was so thick that at times you couldn't move at all. During such a stall, I considered it a private victory when I felt a hand go into my back pocket and quickly pull out, empty. I spun around, but the crowd was so thick there was no obvious suspect and too many obvious suspects all at the same time.

.   .   .

At the train station in Bergerac, Vivian and I got into a van and rode to a large country lodge next to stables where the ride would begin. The other eight or ten riders were all German or Dutch. I can't say that while we were there I learned a single word of either German or Dutch, but I did learn to recognize which one was being spoken. The owner of the lodge, a brooding, quiet man, said that he could trace his family in this area back to the sixteenth century.

As it turned out, most of the other riders were staying in the lodge for the whole week while they took daily excursions out and back on horseback. But Annabelle, the wife of the owner, would lead Vivian and me and a German couple for a randonnée of several days across the countryside. The Germans, Hubertus and Hilda, were both gynecologists, a fact that Vivian and I found curious. We were all mounted on good, strong, trustworthy Andalusian horses. The countryside of rolling hills, forests, and swift rivers was beautiful, and the weather was perfect. We even jumped the horses a time or two, when tree trunks had fallen across our path in the forest. Vivian was thrilled to find that one hotel where we spent the night had ketchup. Once, she was served a whole trout, its head intact. One large eye stared from the plate directly at her. I could tell it was making her uncomfortable. She discreetly covered the eye with a napkin, and then had no appetite for the fish.

During the morning of the second day, we dismounted at the foot of a steep hill and began walking the horses up. It was a little precarious. Hilda had trouble with her horse, which was a recurring theme during the ride. She let it slide back too close to Vivian, who was following behind her. The horse kicked Vivian just above the knee. It hurt, swelled, and stiffened. Fortunately, in the country inn where we stopped for lunch, Madame la Propriétaire showed great concern. She took Vivian into her bedroom and rubbed an analgesic oil called Synthol into the spot by her knee where a bruise was forming. It worked. The pain and the stiffness never got worse. Vivian was walking without trouble the next day, and she was perfumed with a wonderful aroma of camphor from the oil. Synthol isn't sold in the United States. At the end of this trip, and during later trips, Tracy and I always bought several bottles to take back home, where it has eased many minor aches and sore muscles.

The third afternoon, we stopped in Les Eyzies, a village so small that walking from one end to the other takes fifteen minutes at most. But it's at the center of an area that contains a great number of painted caves and other prehistoric sites. The famous painted cave Lascaux is not far away, in Montignac. The Cro-Magnon Rock Shelter, the Abri Cro-Magnon, where the first bones of what scientists now call anatomically modern humans were discovered in 1868, is at the edge of town, behind a hotel near the tiny railroad stop. The Musée National de Préhistoire is also there, having been carved into the steep, rocky cliffs behind the town. Vivian and I visited the museum, then walked along a balcony where Vivian was horrified by a statue she described as "a naked caveman." The balcony looks down on the town and the Vézère River, which makes a huge bend at the town and then runs along a distant row of cliffs to the left. Straight ahead, beyond the river, is a flat plain that stretches to the far horizon. People—anatomically modern humans, which is to say people like us—have been living along these cliffs by that river continuously for twenty-five thousand years or more. It was easy to see why. The cliffs were a barrier, so nothing human or animal could sneak up from behind. Overhangs in the cliffs provided shelter where a well-placed fire would keep marauding animals at bay. There was plenty of water, and the herds of animals who came for water themselves could be seen from the cliffs even when they were far in the distance. Hunting would have been good and food plentiful. And there was something else that I thought would have been important to those distant ancestors and should not be ignored: the scene that lay before us—the curving river, the lush plain, the cliffs to the left far beyond—was beautiful. Long ago, people just like us had chosen to live here. They had had practical reasons for doing so, but I believe they must have had aesthetic ones as well. I didn't know it at the time, but the idea for my second book was born as I stood with Vivian, quietly looking across that verdant landscape.

And it's no surprise to find that Les Eyzies is a popular vacation destination in France, especially for families who enjoy the outdoors. There is good hiking, canoeing, fishing, and camping. The little town swells enormously during July and August. Far to the southeast, in the Ardèche, is a painted cave called

Chauvet, high on a hill that overlooks a river and a natural bridge named Pont d'Arc. That is also a popular vacation destination in the summer. The natural features of a landscape that attracted people in prehistory still attract people today.

The last afternoon, when we stopped at the top of a hill to rest the horses, Vivian walked away to explore a little. A few minutes later, she shouted, "Hey, gang, wild strawberries!" I would not have seen them, but the small plants were everywhere once you knew to look. Their berries were tinier than any I had ever seen, barely the size of green peas. But they produced so much flavor that we ate them one at a time, in order to give each powerful little morsel its due.

The next day, Annabelle drove us to the station where Vivian and I boarded a train for Lyon. We said warm goodbyes. We didn't say so, but all of us assumed that these goodbyes would be forever. But that wasn't the case. By chance I would see Annabelle ten years later, with Tracy.

.   .   .

Tracy and Ben arrived in Lyon a little before Vivian and I did. As our train was pulling in, we could see them waiting for us, surrounded by luggage. Tracy was waving her hand and smiling. Ben was smiling, too, but a little self-consciously. He had his guitar strapped to his back.

We gathered our luggage—thirteen pieces in all!—and waited for the train to Roanne, the small town where Tracy and I had stopped thirteen years before. René, the owner and director of L'École de Trois Ponts, was waiting to meet us at the train. The school was in a medium-sized château technically in the city of Roanne but just on the edge and off enough by itself so that it seemed to be in the country. (The school still exists but in a different château not far away and with different ownership.) Tracy and I had a room, and Ben and Vivian were in separate rooms. All the rooms had large windows that let in plenty of light and were comfortably appointed with antique furniture. We had chosen this school over many other possibilities because it had both language instruction and a cooking school that Tracy was eager to try. The instructor in the cooking school had worked at Les Frères Troisgros.

Learning to speak French was a goal Tracy and I had set for ourselves after our first trip to Paris. She was fluent in Spanish, one of the reasons our maid, Rosie, had bonded so strongly with her. So Tracy thought that learning French would be easy enough. I was under no delusions. I had no ear for languages and had almost not graduated from Rice University because I came close to failing the required upper-level French course. Tracy took two semesters of French at Austin Community College; I worked with a private tutor on Sunday afternoons. When *French in Action* appeared on PBS, Tracy and I became devoted watchers. In our cars, we followed various instructional tapes by repeating phrases as we drove. Despite all that, we didn't make much progress. It's probably more accurate to say that we didn't make any progress at all. If someone spoke French to us, we seldom understood. Nor could we read French with any facility.

Although they never complained, I know now that Ben and Vivian were mildly bored during the two weeks we were there. They dutifully attended their French lessons. They were polite and often charming at meals with the other people at the school, who were all older. But neither Ben nor Vivian was in the mood to learn much French. The only time I heard Ben say a single French word was when we played Ping-Pong each evening, after dinner, and I insisted on keeping score in French. Sometimes the two of them would walk across a pasture to a canal with a footpath running beside it. René had a big, goofy, lovable blond Labrador who liked to tag along. Or, leaving the dog behind, they walked for thirty minutes in the other direction to arrive at the center of town. They were most intrigued by French school supplies, which seemed to them more mature and refined than similar products in the stores at home, especially the notebooks. Their pages were printed in a grid rather than just lined. In fact, it's difficult to find a notebook in France whose pages *aren't* printed in a grid. It's a tiny Gallicism that I'm fond of myself.

Tracy and I, however, were never bored, even for a moment. We happily, almost joyfully, did our homework together. It was like a study date in college, although we really did study. We set about memorizing verb conjugations and quizzed each other on past participles. We knew so little, despite our tapes and other stabs at learning French, that everything we learned now seemed like huge progress.

The chef at the cooking school was a tall, pale man about forty who was slyly funny in his heavily accented English. He was so adept that Tracy found some aesthetic pleasure even in watching him crack an egg. The other students in the cooking class included a couple from Baton Rouge, who were bureaucrats who worked for the state of Louisiana. They had no interest in learning French, but were very interested in cooking. At home, they both had Sunday off; he also had Wednesday off, and she had Saturday. He spent all day Wednesday shopping for and cooking an elaborate meal. They ate leftovers until Saturday, when she spent all day cooking enough for a feast that night and enough more food to last until Wednesday. They spent some time each evening during the week leafing through cookbooks to find new dishes, the more exotic and difficult to prepare the better. Every Saturday and Wednesday night, they went out to dance to Cajun music. Evidently, dancing and cooking formed a perfect balance. They were both slender and radiantly healthy.

One night, they hosted a dance party at the school. They had brought a handful of CDs by Steve Riley and the Mamou Playboys and other Cajun bands. They put one on and started all of us dancing by giving some small bits of instruction here and there. Tracy liked dancing, and I liked dancing, but neither one of us danced well. We hadn't had a lesson since seventh grade. But that night, thanks to some tips from our Cajun friends from Baton Rouge, we were much less bad than usual.

Afterward, as we lay in bed, we talked for a long time about what we wanted our life together to be. We had already been married for twenty years and were looking forward to twenty more, but our marriage was a shared project that we had been making up as we went along. The couple from Baton Rouge lived a different way. All the cooking and the dancing and the comfortable regularity appealed to both of us. In our late-night reverie, we could imagine ourselves living just that way. I would learn to cook, we would both learn to dance, and we wouldn't need anything else. We would have a modest but pleasant, comfortable, and fulfilling life. It didn't sound bad.

"Of course," Tracy said after a pensive silence, "we can't start until Ben and Vivian are out of college." Our new friends had no children. And they both admitted—bragged, actually— that their jobs with the state of Louisiana were not the least bit demanding. I liked my job, but even though I was taking this entire month off to travel, it was demanding and required long hours. And Tracy wanted to make money herself—enough money to support herself if something happened to me, but also for the feeling of independence it would give her. Money always created friction between us. Every eight or ten months, we would make each other angry as we spent a long evening together trying to create a household budget. The next day, with perfect aplomb and implicit mutual consent, we ignored the budget we had argued about the night before and went right back to making things up as we went along.

Being reminded of Ben and Vivian punctured our dream of ourselves as dancing cooks. "I don't really think it's for us after all," Tracy said, not with a sigh but with a short laugh. We decided to enjoy our trip while it lasted and not to worry. We would figure everything out when we got back home.

. . .

The two weeks at the school went rather slowly for Vivian and Ben and quickly for Tracy and me, but none of us were sorry to get on the train for Paris. We had rented an apartment on the rue des Rosiers, in the Marais. Today this whole quarter, and the rue des Rosiers in particular, has blossomed into one of the most chic and trendy areas of Paris. It's filled with small boutiques selling the newest fashions and sleek bars selling artisanal cocktails. If you're walking among the large crowds that are drawn to the area on a Saturday afternoon, it's easy to become convinced that no one in the whole world is older than twenty-three.

But in 1995 it still had vestiges of the large Jewish community who once lived around the rue des Rosiers. The beautiful Art Nouveau Agoudas Hakehilos Synagogue stood at the end of the street. Its rippling, wavy façade was designed by Hector

Guimard, who also designed the curving cast-iron entrances to the Métro. And almost directly across the street from us, Jo Goldenberg's delicatessen was still open and very popular. In 1982, it had been in headlines around the world when terrorists attacked the restaurant with a bomb and machine guns, killing six people and wounding twenty-two others. The attackers weren't identified until more than three decades later. Although that attack had occurred thirteen years before this visit, a reminder of the lingering danger still remained. Heavily armed soldiers in burgundy berets stood guard by the synagogue and routinely patrolled the neighborhood.

Our apartment was on the third floor. The biggest room was the kitchen. It contained a large table, which was the only place to sit in the apartment. The bathroom was next to the kitchen, but it held only a shower and a sink. The toilet was in a small closet right next to the stove, so any delicate need for privacy had to be overcome. There was one very small bedroom, with one very small bed, which Tracy and I took for ourselves. The long, narrow living room overlooked the street. It had two facing couches that served as beds for Vivian and Ben. They both liked to stand at the window, watching people on the street below.

Our first morning there, we set out into Paris and went immediately to the top of the Eiffel Tower. Ben and I had once climbed the steps up the inside of the Statue of Liberty to the crown, but neither one of us was ready to climb now and we gladly took the elevator. We all exclaimed about the view, and it is indeed a nice view, but we all knew that the real purpose of going there was not to enjoy the view but to be able to say that you had been to the top of the Eiffel Tower.

It was impossible to tell what impression the Louvre made

on Ben and Vivian. They dutifully stared at the *Mona Lisa*, but it was surrounded by crowds and difficult to see and impossible to enjoy. Other paintings or sculptures would catch their eye now and then, although only the *Winged Victory*, at the top of the long marble staircase, made a strong impression. Ben spent much of his time looking at two pretty French girls about his age who were happily touring the museum together. I thought they might have been teasing him a little by taking pains to cross his path time and again.

The Rodin Museum, though, was a success. They both knew *The Thinker*, and that gave them a place to start. They saw Rodin's other works as variations on *The Thinker*, which isn't entirely true but not a bad first hypothesis. And the museum is really a house with gardens—a large, impressive house with large, impressive gardens, to be sure, but still recognizably a house. It's a more familiar setting than the cavernous Louvre.

And they liked randomly walking here and there along the streets of Paris. Sometimes, in the afternoon, we let them go out on their own. The first time they did this, as I found out much later, they went straight to a McDonald's and ordered beer. They had done enough of their own research before the trip to discover that McDonald's in Paris served wine and beer, and that the legal drinking age for wine and beer at that time was sixteen.

By chance, we were there for the Fête de la Musique. That Wednesday, June 21, James Brown was giving a free concert at the Place de la République, not too far from the rue des Rosiers. We all wanted to go. As I've mentioned, during the summer in France it doesn't get dark until ten or so. Though the concert probably wouldn't start until then, we walked over shortly after dinner, thinking that if we were early enough we could find a good spot. But every block closer to République the crowd on the sidewalk grew thicker. At the République itself, the crowd was impenetrable. We were stuck at the edge, far from the stage.

Vivian was undaunted: she was convinced that she saw an opening through the crowd that we could use to get closer. With Vivian leading and all of us holding hands in a line behind her, we plunged in. We did penetrate ten yards or so, but then the opening ahead closed and the crowd behind us closed, too. We were stuck and immobile while the crowd around us pulsed with trapped energy. I thought that if I lifted my feet off the ground, I would not fall—I'd be supported by the press of bodies around me.

I had Ben's hand and Tracy's hand. Tracy was holding Vivian's hand. We all gripped as tightly as we could. I realized—in fact, we all realized—that if we lost hold of Ben and Vivian we wouldn't know how to find them again and they wouldn't know where to go or what to do. Just then, a drunken boy about eighteen, wearing a sleeveless T-shirt, started pushing us aggressively from behind, all the while shouting insistently in French. He kept pushing and pushing. He was about to break us apart, so I had no choice. I lowered my shoulder and pushed him back, hard. He hadn't expected that, but he quickly regrouped and came at us again, this time threatening a karate chop where I was holding on to Ben. Again, I had no choice. I let go of Tracy's hand, thinking that this was why I'd done all those early-morning workouts at Richard Lord's Boxing Gym. I hit him as hard as I could with an uppercut to his diaphragm, hoping to knock the wind out of him. I don't know if I did or not, but he did fade back and disappear as the crowd surged around us. That's the only time I've hit anyone in anger in my life. Tracy and Vivian were forcing their way out, and I followed as best I could, pulling Ben behind me. I was near the edge of the crowd when Ben was caught and couldn't budge no matter how hard I pulled. Both our arms were stretched out completely. Six or eight people stood between us, pushing and swaying. I looked at Ben. His eyes were wide with fear and looking directly into mine. I thought that if our grip was broken the crowd would swell around and over him and he would be lost forever. So I held on and held on and pulled, and finally there was a small opening in the crowd and we could move again. Tracy and Vivian were just ahead. We got out of the Place de la République and across a broad boulevard and down another street. There were still people around, but not so many. We stopped for a moment, all breathing heavily. "I guess we're not going to hear James Brown," Vivian said.

We wandered a bit after that. Every small café had music of some sort, and there were plenty of musicians on the street corners, playing blues, jazz, or French chansons. We stopped in one café where a tall, thin woman in a formal gown played lovely classical music on the violin. Away from the milling crowd for James Brown, the night was fresh and easy, with a wonderful air of freedom. We all went to bed happy. We could still hear distant music floating on the night air. The next morning, I went out early to buy croissants for breakfast. It was a mild day with a clear blue sky. I was astonished to see that the streets were completely clean. Workers in the night had hauled the trash away, and every trace of the Fête de la Musiqué had vanished.

One afternoon, we took a train out into the country to see a demanding horseback competition called "eventing" that combines riding cross-country, jumping, and dressage. We got off the train at a small village and walked from there to an immense, rolling meadow where the cross-country course had been erected. We could see four or five of the obstacles, but we couldn't see the whole course. As we stood near the starting line, a rider would take off at a gallop and disappear into the distance, only to reappear several minutes later and confront the obstacles nearer to us. One was a large burning ring the horse had to jump through. Another was a small hill with a fence at the top and a ditch with water on the other side. Still another had two fences, separated by a trench in between; the horse and rider had to clear both fences in a single jump. Each obstacle was more dangerous than anything Vivian or I would ever attempt, but watching these horses and riders take them with aplomb thrilled us, especially seeing the horses fearlessly jump through the burning ring.

When we got on the train back to Paris, heavily armed soldiers were already patrolling the cars. The train made several stops along the way at some of the wretched banlieues north of Paris, where noisy and excited gangs of teenagers and young men boarded. Soon there were shouts back and forth between them and the soldiers, and much jostling from car to car. The news in those days was full of what was called "unrest" in the banlieues, and now we were witnesses to it. All of them, both soldiers and gangs, got off at the Gare du Nord, which had become notorious as a place where the gangs gathered. There had been vandalism, fights, shakedowns, purses snatched, intimidations, and so on. Tracy and I had avoided this station during our visit. We were glad the soldiers had been on the train, and now we waited impatiently for the train to move on, away from the trouble.

But not Ben. He was excited, involved, and really interested for the first time since we had gotten to France. If he had been on his own, he would have gotten off the train to follow the action in the station. He sank back in his seat as the train began to move. He was fourteen. I had not known how much street life, disorder, and defiance all appealed to him. As I looked at him, sitting deflated and disappointed next to Tracy, I became wary of the years ahead. And they were indeed difficult years, although all has ended well.

. . .

During the rest of the trip, we managed to take Ben and Vivian to a few places they really did love. One was the sprawling flea market at the Porte de Clignancourt. Ben studied the old model cars carefully before buying one. Vivian rummaged through vintage clothes. Several times, she held a dress against herself and looked in a mirror, but she resisted buying anything. Seeing the Impressionists and van Gogh at the Musée d'Orsay didn't have quite the appeal of the Rodin Museum but we left the museum happily chatting with one another.

And French cuisine? All of us eating from a tower of seafood at Bofinger and sharing a carafe of white wine was a feast beyond anything they had ever imagined. Bouillon Chartier was an even better experience. It's a famous restaurant Tracy had read about before our first visit. She wanted to return every time we came to Paris, so of course we took Ben and Vivian there, too. Bouillon Chartier was founded in 1896, and its décor still evokes that era. The restaurant is one cavernous room brightly lit by brass chandeliers with lights inside white glass bowls. The long tables have red-and-white tablecloths that are covered with long strips of white butcher paper. On the walls are large mirrors mounted in dark wood. The floor is white tile. Originally, it was a cheap restaurant intended for laborers, tradesmen, and starving artists. In keeping with that tradition, the menu is basically a very long list of traditional French dishes, still at reasonable prices.

The waiters all wear white shirts, black vests, and white aprons. Ours arrived quickly. Ben and Vivian were amazed and fascinated when he wrote our order on the white butcher paper on our table with a crayon. The food arrived only moments later. It was hot, and there was plenty of it, and it tasted fine, but it had obviously been spooned onto our plates out of vats on the stoves in the kitchen. The attraction of Chartier is the place itself rather than the cuisine. The waiters are part of the show. They sometimes bring out as many as seven plates—not on trays, but balanced in a line along one arm. When we were finished, our waiter used the same crayon to add up our bill on the butcher paper, again delighting Vivian and Ben.

I haven't gone back there by myself, but I'm reminded of Chartier constantly when I'm in Paris. I still have my Michelin map of the city. It's a blue perfect-bound book a little longer and a little wider than a number-ten envelope. That particular map has been out of print for years. I purchased my copy in 1992 and have brought it with me to Paris on every trip since. I guard it carefully for two reasons. One, I find it very useful and convenient. The maps are clear and accurate, and the book is filled with other information, such as museum addresses and a Métro map; yet it's small enough to slip easily into my jacket pocket. The second reason is that on the map on page nineteen there is a circle drawn in pencil at 7 rue du Faubourg Montmartre and the word "Chartier," also in pencil, in Tracy's handwriting.

· · ·

We were never idle, and really saw a lot of Paris in the week we were there. Everyone was happy, or at least happy enough. But the possibilities of Paris didn't seem to lure either of our children the way they did Tracy and me. Neither Tracy nor I was entirely convinced that they saw that there *were* possibilities in Paris. But at times in the following years we saw signs that the trip had affected them more than it seemed to have at the time. Even now, Vivian can see the excruciatingly chic saleswoman with sleek black hair wearing a yellow shift dress who waited on her and Tracy in one boutique. Both Tracy and I at different times heard Ben tell a friend, "When we were living in France . . ."

CHAPTER SIX

The Crypt of Quentin Roosevelt

Tracy and I routinely forgot our wedding anniversary, which was in late September. Even now I don't remember the exact date. But we always remembered the year—1975. It was in October or November 1995, the year we had taken Ben and Vivian to France for the month of June, that we realized that we had let our twentieth anniversary go by without any notice. What should we do? That was a simple question to answer—we would go to Paris. But since Thanksgiving and Christmas were arriving soon, and since we had been in Paris just a few months earlier, we decided to wait and return to Paris the following spring. We could afford to go because I had another, unlikely form of permission.

For well over a decade, magazine business took me to New York up to fifteen times a year. I always stayed at the Waldorf-Astoria, an indulgence that stopped abruptly when I left *Texas Monthly* and had to pay for hotel rooms in New York with my own money. The Waldorf is a Hilton hotel. I joined Hilton Honors, their loyalty program, and by the spring of 1996 I had enough points in my account so we could stay twelve nights in the Paris Hilton for free. But when I tried to make our reservations, the hotel refused: they said they reserved only a few rooms for Honors points, and those rooms were already taken during the dates of our stay.

In the course of reporting many stories, I had learned a few subterfuges that were useful for getting around barriers. For instance, if you were having trouble contacting the boss of an organization, call on the weekend. The person who answers will be the boss. I decided to write directly to the president of Hilton. It was a polite and respectful letter, saying that my wife and I had counted on celebrating our anniversary in Paris, using my Honors points. Was there a way he could help? I said I would remain a loyal Hilton customer whatever he decided. All of this had the virtue of being true. He wrote back that this one time and this one time only he would see to it that the Paris hotel would make an exception.

He must have done something more than that. When Tracy and I arrived, the desk clerk immediately got on her phone and a smartly dressed woman came out of a back office to escort us to our room. It turned out to be bright, spacious, and luxurious. There was a living room with a couch, several chairs, a desk, and a large television. The bedroom had a king-sized bed and a vanity table for Tracy, and the bathroom had both a shower and a large tub. There was an impressive bouquet of flowers in the living room, a smaller one in the bedroom, and a basket filled with fruit and chocolates. The woman left us her card in case we should need anything else. I sent the president of Hilton our thanks on a postcard of the Eiffel Tower, which was very close and visible through our windows.

The hotel, which is still there although no longer a Hilton, was on the rue Jean Rey, just to the west of the Eiffel Tower, near the Avenue de Suffren. That street runs southeast, paral-

lel with the Champ de Mars, and soon meets the Avenue de
la Motte–Picquet. The Swiss Village is near this intersection,
a collection of high-end galleries and antique-furniture stores
where Tracy enjoyed browsing as if it were a museum. Most
of the items for sale were too expensive or too bulky to take
home in our suitcases, but to my surprise she kept returning
to a wooden chess set. It was a folding oak box with tiny brass
hinges and a brass clasp. The pieces, also oak, fit inside the box.
They were hand carved. The eyes of one knight were slightly
crossed; one queen listed subtly to the side. The white pieces
were natural wood, the black pieces stained a deep auburn.
When open and turned upside down, the top and bottom of the
box became a board in which the alternating natural and stained
squares were skillfully inlaid, as was a thin border with an intricate design. Tracy had no interest in chess, although she knew
that I had played seriously and unsuccessfully when I lived in
San Francisco during my early twenties. But she admired the
craftsmanship behind this set and liked the way it looked, especially the contrasting colors of the wood. We bought it. It was
expensive, but not quite an extravagance, and it was an object
we both liked. The saleswoman taped bubble wrap around the
box, which made it safely home in our luggage.

At the intersection of Suffren and La Motte–Picquet, we
found what became our favorite restaurant in Paris. The restaurant there now is comfortable and pleasant, but different
from the one Tracy and I enjoyed so much. That restaurant
had offered a prix fixe menu with a multitude of choices for the
entrée, the plat, and the dessert, *plus* a generous carafe of wine.
It had a cozy, neighborhood-clubhouse atmosphere. At many
of the tables, beloved family dogs lay patiently at the feet of the
diners.

We often ordered dishes from the prix fixe menu without knowing what they were. One night, the waiter placed a hot bowl in front of each of us that was filled with tiny seashells. They looked like two bowls of steaming pearls. Then, with some ceremony, the waiter carefully set a cork from a wine bottle with twenty or thirty straight pins stuck in it on the table between us. Then he disappeared without a word.

Tracy and I looked at our bowls of tiny shells. Were we supposed to eat these shells? How? Tracy picked up the cork and looked more closely at the straight pins before setting it back on the table. "I have no idea," she said. I didn't, either.

We were seated at a banquette. At the table beside us, a distinguished gentleman in a dark suit and tie was dining alone. Or almost alone. His floppy-eared dog sat with its head on the man's lap, hoping for some crumbs. I asked him to forgive me for bothering him but, holding up the cork with the pins, I asked, "Qu'est-ce que c'est?"

"Une épingle," he said. He took one of the pins out of the cork and one of the shells from my bowl, stuck the pin into the shell, and extracted a tiny sliver of white meat. I thanked him. Tracy and I, armed with pins, attacked the shells. It was not always easy to get the meat out of the shell, but the little slivers were filled with flavor. They were a real delicacy that we were forced to eat slowly, one by one. They were coquina clams, I later found out.

We went to the horse races at Longchamp—officially the Hippodrome ParisLongchamp—in the Bois de Boulogne. The track at Longchamp was not dirt, as most tracks are in the United States. Instead, it had the most beautiful, iridescent green grass, whose soft footing the horses seemed to love. They run the races clockwise   not counterclockwise, as in America—and you can bet only to win or place: there's no show betting. The paddock is behind the grandstand. A fenced lane leads from there to the track. For a while, we stood right where the lane met the track. The horses walked as they left the paddock, but as soon as they were on the turf of the track, the jockeys asked for a gallop. It didn't take much with these horses—usually just a nudge with boot heels against their flanks was sufficient—and they would sprint away down the track almost soundlessly. In *A Moveable Feast*, Hemingway writes about going to this very track with his wife, Hadley, and how happy they were there. Hemingway did better with his bets than I did with mine, or so he says, but Tracy and I were just as happy. We drank champagne and ate tartes aux pommes as we watched the horses run on the grass.

I had met a German woman on a randonnée across Bordeaux. Her husband worked in the German Embassy, which was right by our hotel. They invited us to their house one evening for dinner. They lived in a comfortable suburb west of Paris. The nicer neighborhoods and suburbs of Paris are generally in the west. The prevailing winds blow west to east. In the days when Parisians burned coal for heat, smoke and ash blew from the bourgeois west into the eastern, less desirable arrondissements.

We rode a commuter train for about thirty minutes and found their address a short walk from the small train station. It was a white two-story wooden-framed house with green shutters. There was a large, neatly trimmed yard. Flower beds lined the walk to the front door. This house and yard would not have seemed out of place in our neighborhood in Austin. We had blanquette de veau, very well prepared by him. Since he was a diplomat, they had lived in several different countries, including the United States. As a young man in the late 1960s, he had even attended the University of Kansas in Lawrence, not far from Kansas City. He remembered John Riggins dragging would-be tacklers into the end zone; that was a name I could never have predicted would come up that evening. Their two teenaged sons had traveled with them when they were younger, but now both boys were in a boarding school in Germany. He showed us some work he was doing on the second floor that was made more difficult because it was seldom easy to find where the French carpenters had run the electrical wires. In Germany, he said, they all went at predictable right angles. Like Tracy, she enjoyed gardening, and showed us her impressive vegetable garden behind the house. The evening was as pleasant and relaxed as if we were old friends. When it was time to leave, he said he would drive us to the hotel. No, no, we said. That wasn't necessary. We were happy to take the train. "Well," he said, "I am going to drive into Paris right now. You can come with me or not, as you choose." I thought it was such a refined way of insisting. We conceded, and happily let him drive us to the hotel.

In our room, I poured two glasses of wine and we switched on the television. We had had a television in the hotel in Roanne, although we'd never turned it on, but we had never had one in our room in Paris before. We enjoyed it far more than we would have predicted. This night, what should we find playing but *Austin City Limits*. In those days, the program was not yet the great success it has since become. It was smaller-scale and taped in a studio on the University of Texas campus. Tracy and I went from time to time, but we had six or eight friends who were regulars at the tapings. And there they were, smiling and clapping for the music, as we watched them from our hotel in Paris. We could have been in our own living room at home.

Later, while Tracy was in the bathroom getting ready for bed, I switched to a German sports channel, which was showing boxing live from Munich. Between rounds, when I saw the boxers in their corners, I called out, "Tracy, come here and look."

"What is it?"

"You have to come see."

A few moments later, she came into the living room wearing a white terrycloth robe provided by the hotel. I pointed to the television screen without saying anything. "Ha!" she let out and started laughing. There, working as a second in the corner of one of the boxers, was Richard Lord, our friend from Austin. I had been going to his gym three times a week for at least fifteen years. Tracy and I had attended his wedding only a few weeks before leaving for Paris.

Tracy sat next to me on the couch as we watched Richard's boxer fighting valiantly against a stronger opponent. I said, "When people ask us what we did in Paris, we can say we watched live boxing from Munich on television."

"No, we can't say that," she said. "They'll be too jealous."

"Well, they should be." Tracy laughed, but I could indeed see reasons why they should be jealous. I had been thinking about the evening we had just spent together. The dinner with our German friends was much like a dinner we might have had in Austin. It was mere chance that it had been near Paris. The friendliness and the companionship were more important than the location and would have been the same no matter where we were. Of course, there had been some tense moments for us on the way to the hotel, when our German friend drove into the churning sea of vehicles circling L'Étoile. That was unique to Paris. But then, once we were safely in our room, we found our friends in Austin appearing on television. Now we were sitting on a couch, transfixed, watching Richard, whom we saw regularly anyway. Had we come to Paris for this? Well, maybe we had, although not *just* for this. Of course, there was plenty to see and do that can be seen and done only in Paris. But it was also very nice to be sitting together on the couch, feeling calm and happy and among friends. Though Paris offered opportunities, it made no demands. We could sit there for as long as we wanted, and that felt very Parisian to us both. The experiences we had had that evening had affected us both in exactly the same way, which was not always true at home—we would not have both sat watching Richard at home. Doing so felt very Parisian, too, part of life in a homey, domestic Paris that we had found in a Hilton hotel where we would never have thought to look. I ran my fingers through Tracy's hair and kissed her hand, which I was holding in mine.

"I feel sorry for Richard's boxer," she said. He had just lost a close decision.

"I do, too," I said, "but maybe that means that it's time to turn off the TV."

"Okay, chéri. I think it's time."

"Oui, chérie. It's time."

. . .

If I think back about our marriage looking for imperfections, which I don't often do, I suppose I could find more than a few. Some would be temporary. The disagreements, disputes, misunderstandings, and other aggravations that I mentioned earlier would appear and last for only a moment, or for several moments, or for a day, or occasionally even longer than that before they were resolved, usually by one of us giving in to the other. Sometimes, especially when we were first married, these reconciliations were very sweet. But other problems weren't resolved so neatly. They simply faded into the background as our lives continued and were never really resolved. One of these problems was her smoking.

I had been a smoker myself when we married. I had smoked since college. But I began getting frequent nasty and persistent sinus infections and horrible chest congestion. When I gave up smoking, those problems disappeared. I didn't like having ambient smoke in the house while the children were growing, but Tracy had continued smoking even when she was pregnant. Two of the children had serious asthma problems. One evening, I pressed her about quitting more strongly than usual. It threw her into an icy rage, and she didn't speak to me the rest of the evening or the next morning. That evening, I asked her if she was going to speak to me ever again. "I don't know," she said, the first words she had said to me in more than twenty-four hours. I realized then that I could have a wife who smoked or, if I pressed too hard too often, I could have an ex-wife who smoked, so I relented. I occasionally nagged her a little, even so. Sometimes, when she pulled out a cigarette while we were in the car, which I particularly hated, she would look at me with her lighter in her hand and say, "Don't you say a word."

Money caused tension between us as well, as it does in most marriages. But in our case the tension wasn't caused by the lack of money. We weren't starving, and we had a nice house. And we had gotten good investment advice from a friend who was a financial planner. We both felt comfortable with the amount we were saving for college for the children, and for ourselves later on. We didn't need to talk much about the amount of money we had, or how we were using it. The problem for her was that our money all came from my salary. She had no independent source of income, and this made her feel vulnerable if something should happen to me. I didn't have any answer for that.

But our regard for each other was stronger than either of those problems, and certainly stronger than lesser problems. One of the strongest bonds, as I have already mentioned, was the way we often knew without saying a word that we were both thinking the same thing. We could look at each other across a room, our faces expressionless except for our eyes, and we could hear the same thoughts in our heads. This happened often at dinners out, particularly when we could see each other across the table at charity events or social gatherings where we might know the others seated with us only slightly.

One Sunday afternoon, we flew to Dallas, where there was a welcoming party for an old friend of Tracy's who was moving back there from New York. We took a cab from the airport to the party. We had been there perhaps fifteen minutes, certainly no longer than that, when we saw each other across the room, and I knew what she was thinking. I walked over to her and said, "Let's not take time to say goodbye."

"Let's not," she said. We were out the door and on the sidewalk in an instant. The smugness and self-satisfaction of the people there had quickly offended us both. But we had forgotten that we didn't have a car. It was going to be a long walk from this classy residential part of Dallas to the airport. This was long before cell phones, but we both preferred the walk, however long, to going back into the party and asking to use the phone. We shared a delicious feeling of having foiled a conspiracy against us.

We got to Mockingbird Lane, usually a rather busy street, but it was quiet now, on Sunday afternoon. Then, as if on cue, an empty taxi came along. We flagged him down. No one flags down a taxi anywhere in Dallas, ever. We could tell that the grizzled old driver was intensely curious about why two folks dressed in fancy clothes happened to be walking along Mockingbird Lane just then and needed a taxi. "You two out for a stroll?" he ventured.

"No," I said. "We're just going to the airport."

He looked back at us in the rearview mirror, but must have sensed the futility of asking us why we had been walking to the airport, which was several miles away. I left things hanging there, settled back in the seat, and looked over at Tracy. We were both enjoying the little air of mystery we provoked by not letting him know.

Another strong bond between us was our routine. Neither of us liked chaos. We had grown up in families that were orderly, on the whole, and we both wanted order in our own lives as well. If we agreed to meet at a certain time, we were there at that time. If either of us was late, that was unsettling, because it meant that something unforeseen and therefore most likely bad had occurred. Our marriage would have been spared many anxious moments of waiting while imagining the worst if cell phones had been invented sooner. We both liked to keep things neat. We both liked nice clothes. We didn't disagree about raising the children. She was better at it than I was, and though she asked for my opinion, she was the one who made the decisions. She was a very good mother, and all four children adored her. And she and I talked to each other every evening before dinner with a drink, while the children were in their rooms. Often I came home for lunch to be with her while the children were in school.

.   .   .

Tracy's grandfather Elmer Lewis had been a romantic figure as a young man: he was one of the first American military pilots. When Tracy and I married, he was still alive, and so was his adored wife, Aida. Their house was just down the street from the house where Tracy grew up. Once, when we were in Amarillo on a visit, we walked down to see them. Everyone in the family knew that Aida was no longer in the present. At the same time, everyone in the family conceded that Elmer was slightly, although lovably, crazed. He spent his mornings running a filling station alone, and his afternoons tending a hydroponic garden behind his house. During the whole visit, he lectured me happily on hydroponics, looking as if he thought I was going to pick up a trowel that second.

The family still had photographs of Elmer while he was in flight training in San Antonio at the dawn of World War I. He was very handsome in his leather flying helmet and mustache. Quentin Roosevelt, the youngest of Theodore Roosevelt's four sons, was in the same training class as Elmer. The young Roosevelt was charismatic, funny, popular with his fellow pilots, and brave to a fault. He was shot down in combat in 1918. His death was a bitter blow to Elmer, who later named his first son—Tracy's father—after him.

Elmer always told his son, and Quentin Lewis later told Tracy, that Quentin Roosevelt was buried, along with many other heroes of the Great War, in a crypt in a small church in

Paris. That turned out not to be true. Quentin Roosevelt was first buried in Chamery, France, not far from where he was shot down. Then, in 1955, his remains were moved to the Normandy American Cemetery and placed next to his brother Theodore, Jr., who died of a heart attack while fighting in World War II. I learned all that on the Internet. In those days before the Internet, I am certain that some not-too-difficult research in a library would have revealed the truth, but neither Tracy nor I saw any reason to doubt the family legend. While we were in Paris, she wanted above all to visit Quentin Roosevelt's crypt and photograph it for her father and grandfather.

I can no longer find the name of the church and cannot remember where it was, except that it was definitely on the Right Bank, stuck on a quiet corner on a quiet street in a quiet neighborhood. Inside the church, we were met with emptiness, darkness, and silence. We were the only visitors. All the pews were empty, and the confessionals were empty, too. Tracy and I wandered around for a few moments, not knowing what to do, until Tracy saw a crack of light below a door in an otherwise dark stone wall. We both hesitated, looked at each other, and then shrugged. She knocked on the door.

It was certainly not five minutes before there was any response. It was probably not even one minute, but it seemed much longer as we stood there waiting. Finally, the door cracked open and a man's pale, almost translucent face appeared in the gap. He had downy white hair that hung in bangs over his forehead. He was wearing a white priestly robe. He looked back and forth between Tracy and me and then said, "Oui?"

There was a short beat when we were all three silent. But Tracy had courage and charm and determination. In New York in the late 1980s and '90s, there was a kind of warehouse on the Upper West Side that sold the most useful and rare kitchen equipment, as well as dishes, pots, bowls, and so on. But the man who ran it was widely known as difficult, if not impossible. Tracy went there with friends who were amazed when she stood up to him in a kindly but firm manner and soon had him running around the store and up and down ladders, bringing her items and hoping to please her.

Something like that happened now. In hit-and-miss French, but with great enthusiasm and broad smiles, she tried to explain that we were there to find the crypt of Quentin Roosevelt.

"Qui?" he asked. By now he had opened the door farther, revealing the cell where he had been working. A lamp stood by a tall desk with thin legs, on which an ancient, illustrated Bible was open. The priest must have been sitting on the spindly chair in front of the desk. Tracy took a small spiral notebook from her purse, wrote QUENTIN ROOSEVELT in block letters, and handed the paper to the priest. He held it close to his eyes and regarded it carefully, as if he were studying a medieval text. At one point, he looked up, first at me and then at Tracy, and then returned to the sheet of paper. At last, he crooked a finger for us to follow him. He led us to a wall in the church that was covered with white marble rectangles. Each one had a carved name and a date and place of death; some also had a date and location of birth. They didn't seem to be in any particular order. The priest gestured toward them all, turned up his hands, and shrugged. "Pas ici," he said. Not here. We carefully studied each name on the wall, but the priest was right: Quentin Roosevelt was not there. We thanked him profusely, said our farewells, and re-emerged from the church into the sunlight.

We paused for a moment to let our eyes adjust to the bright day, then looked around, trying to decide where to go next.

Tracy was very slightly, almost invisibly agitated, but I could see it in the way she readjusted the strap of her purse over her shoulder and rubbed her hands. "You know what?" she said at last. "I'm going to tell Granddad we saw Quentin Roosevelt's crypt, but it was too dark to take a photograph."

"We did try as hard as we could," I said.

"But I'm not going to say that we *tried* to find it. I'm going to say that we found it." And that is exactly what she told her grandfather Elmer.

Perhaps that is one way the legends of Paris are born.

CHAPTER SEVEN

Monsieur le Président

In 1997 I found an outfitter who offered a hunt for stags in his catalogue. Actually, there would be two hunts, one on Wednesday and one on Saturday. The fee included five nights at the Hôtellerie du Bas-Bréau in Barbizon, near the Forest of Fontainebleau, just an hour and a quarter by automobile from Paris. A stag hunt sounded like such an adventure that I couldn't resist, especially after a well-traveled friend told us that the Bas-Bréau was his favorite place in all the world.

We stayed in Paris for a few days before going on to Barbizon. One nagging question was what I would wear on the hunt. The outfitter had given me the name of someone to call who had been on a hunt. "Don't worry about it," he told me. "No matter what you wear, you will be underdressed." I had breeches and black riding boots that came up to my knees, a blazer, and black gloves. But I needed, or I thought I needed, a white shirt with something called a stock tie. By chance, on the evening following our arrival in Paris, we saw a place where we thought we could find one.

That night, we attended a performance of Molière's *Le Malade imaginaire* at La Comédie Française. There is a lot of theater in Paris, perhaps even more than in New York, and it goes mostly unnoticed by American visitors because of the language barrier. But Tracy and I enjoyed going if we could read the play in English before we went, and we especially liked La Comédie Française. It is directly descended from Molière's seventeenth-century company and is still in the same place, on the rue de Richelieu, near the Palais Royale. Molière collapsed onstage while playing the lead in *Le Malade imaginaire* and died shortly afterward. He was so thoroughly theatrical that he even died on cue. The chair he was sitting in at that moment is preserved in the prop room of La Comédie.

We had both read the play in English. We had a copy in French besides, although the play is more than three hundred years old and the language was often opaque to us, despite all our efforts at learning French. Entering the theater made us feel that we were in these moments very much a part of Paris. The curtain was red velvet, as were the carpet and the seat covers. That alone seemed to take us into a different world. Everyone in the audience looked confident and sophisticated as they all chatted softly in lilting French. We had dressed nicely and bought good seats on the ground, about eight rows back from the stage. Tracy was the prettiest woman there. She attracted some admiring glances before the lights went down and the curtain parted. I'm sure she didn't notice. She liked for me or the children to tell her that she looked lovely, but she didn't expect it and certainly didn't need it from the rest of the world.

Le Malade was perfect, down to the smallest detail. The sets were spare but created the illusion of being in the seventeenth century. They even had a reproduction of Molière's chair where the malade sat. (At least, I presume it was a reproduction, and not the chair itself.) The female lead looked beautiful in a satin robe trimmed with lace, and the male lead was dashing indeed in a leather tunic and tall boots, with a sword hanging by his side. The acting was so good that we thought we could have followed the plot even if we hadn't read the play. These thoughts were perhaps more prideful than true, but we found ourselves laughing on cue with the rest of the audience; we were far from bewildered. Unlike most modern productions, this version of *Le Malade* also included the dance and musical interludes between the acts and after the final scene, which were written for the play by one of Molière's colleagues. That's the way it was originally performed, and that night the interludes completed the illusion of being transported from the present to three hundred years in the past.

As Tracy and I left the theater, holding hands and almost literally floating into the night, we saw an imposing store right next door that completed the illusion of time travel into the past. The store sold everything one might need for la chasse— hunting of all kinds but stag hunting in particular. The windows displayed a collection of swords and circular brass horns and other anachronisms, and nothing remotely contemporary.

When we went there the next morning, we discovered that to this store hunting was an expensive, clubby, gentlemanly sport. The more time it took and the more money it cost to prepare for the hunt, the better. The first floor had rows of gleaming shotguns along the walls, field clothes of thick wool, and an immense variety of knives in glass cases. All the gear for stag hunting was down a wide, thickly carpeted marble staircase. Everything in the room seemed to be from centuries ago. There were black leather boots that came up over the knee, and long brocade coats with embroidered edges. Circular racks were covered with three-cornered hats. Several other racks were

devoted to shining brass horns with circular bases. Eight or
ten long, straight swords in scabbards lay on an ornate wooden
table. Everything in the room was a radiantly new anachro-
nism. Tracy laughed out loud.

An affable salesman appeared. I told him I was going on a
hunt and wondered what I needed. He advised against a coat.
A hunt is a private club, and each club has its colors, and since I
didn't belong to a club, there wasn't any point in having a coat.
That was welcome news: the coats were so expensive I wouldn't
have bought one anyway. I didn't want a horn, although I did
buy a CD of hunting calls—that's how hunters communicate
when they are spread out across a forest. And they didn't have
boots in my size. I wished I could have tried a pair on. Finally,
I settled for a pair of white crocheted riding gloves and a white
stock collar. Back at our hotel, Tracy surprised me with a small
box from the store that had been wrapped as a present. Inside,
I found a pocket knife made by the French manufacturer Nontron. Somehow she had bought the knife and had it wrapped
without my seeing her. The knife had one long, sharp blade
and a shorter can-and-bottle opener. On the back was a hinged
corkscrew. The wooden handle was decorated with a symbol
from one of France's Paleolithic caves. I carried the knife for
years. We shared many bottles of wine that I opened with its
corkscrew.

We left Paris the next morning. When we arrived at the
Bas-Bréau, we could see why our well-traveled friend had
called it his favorite place in all the world. It's a country lodge
of wooden beams and stucco, surrounded by immaculate gardens. Its restaurant has been a desirable destination for decades.
Our room had a large, comfortable bed partially set back into

a recess in the wall. The bedspread had a blue-and-white floral design that matched the heavy drapes.

The married couple who owned the hotel were also stag hunters. Neither Tracy nor I hunted, nor had our families hunted, although Tracy, as a daughter of Amarillo, always proudly claimed that she was a good shot. I have a photograph of her in high school wearing plaid Bermuda shorts and holding a revolver with a long barrel among a group of friends who are holding rifles. They had all been target shooting. We were once invited for a weekend at a friend's ranch where we could shoot skeet. Sure enough, she regularly blasted the clay pigeons out of the sky.

Tracy stayed behind during the first hunt, on Wednesday. Late in the afternoon, I got tangled in the branch of a tree, came off my horse, and fell hard against its rising left front knee. Although occasionally a trickle of blood ran out of the corner of my mouth, I managed to finish the hunt. Then two hunters loaded me into a car, and in a few moments we were racing through villages and down back roads between rolling fields. In a quarter-hour, we stopped in front of an ugly stucco building on a side street in a charmless village. A receptionist showed us into a large room. There was a wooden desk in one corner, a wooden examining table covered with white paper in another corner, a sink, and a few cabinets. Almost immediately the doctor burst into the room and shooed my two companions out. He was a large man, about fifty years old, with huge, thick shoulders, an ample belly, and a round, fleshy face sporting a bushy mustache. He motioned for me to lie down on the examining table.

In French, he asked if my teeth were all right. They were.

Had I had a tetanus shot recently? I thought so but wasn't sure. Was I hurt anywhere else? No. He nodded, and then, beginning at my neck, he moved his hands slowly down my body, pressing here and there, particularly around my stomach. He repeatedly asked if I felt any pain. I didn't.

Abruptly, he took my lip between his thumb and forefinger, pulled it out, and peered inside. Then he swabbed out the wound and put a roll of gauze between my lip and teeth. He motioned for me to get up and went to the door to call my companions back in. He said I needed stitches all right, but he didn't have the right apparatus to do the procedure. We would need to go to a hospital in Joigny, a larger town nearby. His charge would be 140 francs, about twenty-five dollars at that time. Fortunately, I had a two-hundred-franc note in my coat. I gave it to the doctor. He sat down behind his desk and pulled out the middle drawer. Papers, pencils, and little tin boxes slid back and forth. He threw my two hundred francs in and rummaged around in the drawer, looking under papers and flipping through the pages of pamphlets, until he found three twenty-franc notes, which he handed to me. Then he shook hands all around and we went our way.

Joigny is a thriving town on the Yonne River. We found the hospital without difficulty and went in the emergency entrance. There was a square room, enclosed in glass, where six young women dressed in white were sitting or standing in relaxed attitudes and joking among themselves, as emergency-room staffs do everywhere. One woman asked if we played in a band. This confused me until I remembered we were still wearing our riding habits. Since I had the wad of gauze in my mouth, one of the other hunters explained what had happened. This produced more jokes and laughter. One of the women handed me a short form to complete. I wrote down my name and the address of the hotel in Barbizon, and, with a shrug of my shoulders, checked that, yes, I had had a recent tetanus shot. In two medical visits to people who had never seen me before, that was all the paperwork I had to do.

Two of the women showed me into an adjoining treatment area, where I took off my riding jacket and lay back on a table. Supremely confident and reassuring, they took the gauze out of my mouth and swabbed my wounds with antiseptic and spread a local anesthetic on my lip. It took effect quickly, and they began sewing me up. I could feel a slight tug on my lips with each stitch, but nothing more. In five days, I could have the stitches removed. And payment? Oh, it would take them a day or so to get the bill out. They would send it to my hotel. Their casualness about everything, especially money, was astonishing to me. I left the hospital with a row of four stitches on my lower lip and another four stitches between my lip and my chin, where my teeth had cut completely through. The bill did arrive two days later. It was about fifty dollars.

Someone had phoned the hotel about my accident, and Tracy was waiting for me in our room when I got back to the Bas-Bréau. She was full of sympathy and had already prepared an icepack for my mouth. She started a warm bath, then helped me pull off my boots and get out of my riding clothes. She washed off my back and sat on the edge of the tub while I soaked. Any injury or illness opened Tracy's huge reservoir of compassion. We went to dinner, but I couldn't eat anything except for some vanilla ice cream. When I tried a sip of wine, it felt as if I'd put a burning coal on my stitches.

We spent Thursday in the gardens of the hotel and exploring Barbizon. On Friday, we walked farther and found the field just on the edge of town where Millet had painted both *The Gleaners* and *The Angelus*. The field, although apparently featureless, was nevertheless recognizable from the paintings. I think it was because of the way the field met the horizon in the distance.

Along the way, we passed a small house with a brass plaque by the door that indicated a doctor's office. I thought that maybe he could remove my stitches, so we wouldn't have to go all the way back to Joigny. We entered the office. As is often the case in France, especially in the small towns, his waiting room was also his family's living room. There was a couch, several stuffed chairs, and a television, although it wasn't on. An elderly woman in a gray shawl was sitting in one of the chairs and greeted us pleasantly. Tracy and I sat on the couch. A few moments later, a bald man with shiny pink cheeks came in, clutching a cap in his hands. He greeted the old woman and us and sat down himself. It was easy to see what they both were thinking: Who could we be? Why were we there?

After another five minutes or so, a stout woman in jeans came in. She almost tripped over a chair because she couldn't stop staring at us. Then the office door opened, and a woman with a cane came out, followed by the doctor, a slight, fair-skinned man with close-cropped dark hair. He, too, stared at us as the woman in the gray shawl went into his office. We waited in absolute silence without moving. All of us in the waiting room looked like wax figures in a museum.

Fifteen minutes later, the elderly woman left the doctor's office, and it was our turn. We made our introductions and shook hands. He seated us in two chairs in front of his desk and then sat down facing us. I told him what had happened and asked about the stitches. I thought he would come take a look, but he didn't. Oh, he said, it was much too early to take them out. I should leave them for at least ten days. We could return then and he would take them out. I told him we were leaving for home next Sunday. He shrugged, smiled, and pleasantly said, "Then I guess I won't take them out." He stood up and said there would be no charge; seeing us had been his pleasure. Good day, madame, monsieur. Good day, doctor.

As Tracy and I left, we saw that several more people had arrived in the office. We felt their stares as we walked through the door and closed it behind us. Out on the street, we both felt oddly exhilarated. We laughed like delinquents who had pulled off an inspired prank. I bent to kiss her, but she put up her hand. "Careful," she said. "Your stitches."

"I think it's all right," I said, and very gently touched my lips to hers.

(Five days later, back in Austin, I made an appointment with a doctor who is a friend of long standing but whom I'd never seen as a patient. At his office, I had to complete endless forms about my health, medical history, and insurance coverage. Payment, I couldn't help noticing, was due at the end of the visit. His office overflowed with patients, but eventually I got in. He had the stitches out in a minute or two. He said he wanted to hear about our trip, but just then he was pressed for time and had to move on. Still, I couldn't resist asking him just one question: had they done a good job sewing up my mouth? "Oh, hell, yes," he said. "A real good job.")

.   .   .

The hunt on Saturday, in the Forest of Fontainebleau, was a much grander affair than the first one. There were more riders, more horses, and more packs of hounds. And this time Tracy could come, too, in a car. At nine o'clock, Madame and Monsieur, who owned the hotel, drove us to a nearby town, where about thirty hunters and hunt followers were already eating massive breakfasts of scrambled eggs, ham, potatoes, fruit, pastries, coffee, and wine. Monsieur advised Tracy and me to do the same: we wouldn't eat again until dinner that evening. The hunters all wore black velvet coats with blue-and-white collars and hems, the insignia of their club. Then we drove to a clearing in the forest where several long horse trailers were parked. Many of the hunters were already there. A few of the men had brass horns slung over one shoulder. Others wore long, straight swords such as we had seen in the store. Many people who weren't hunters stood around the periphery of the clearing. Some had bicycles or small motor scooters; others had come in cars. These were "les suiveurs"—people from the farms and villages nearby who thought following the hunt was great sport.

Scouts had been in the forest early in the morning to catch sight of the stag, follow his movements, and find a place where the hounds could pick up his scent. As the hunters waited in a semicircle, the scouts reported to Monsieur le Président of the hunt, an older gentleman with an almost fierce demeanor. He didn't ride anymore himself—too many falls over the years— but his skill at hunting was still respected. There was much conversation between him and the scouts. Then Monsieur le Président gave instructions. I didn't understand a word of all this. Tracy, meanwhile, was busy taking photographs. It was too good an opportunity to miss. Except for the suiveurs, who were in modern dress, everyone else looked as if they had just come from an audience with Louis XIV. Madame from the hotel took me to my mount, a huge animal, the biggest horse by far that I'd ever ridden. He had once been a trotter at the track. Tracy was going to ride in a car with Monsieur le Président and two of his cronies.

She told me later that they were very gallant toward her and spoke to her in fractured English but with great respect. The mood in the car eased a bit when the three men realized that she couldn't understand their French. They talked freely among themselves after that and often shook with laughter. Tracy was sure their talk was full of ribaldry. The car bounced and swerved as the president guided it down lanes through the forest.

Meanwhile, I was holding my own, keeping up with the hunters. Once, I saw the stag, about a hundred yards away. He had come into a clearing, paused to look at us, then bounded back into the forest and disappeared. We trailed after him for several hours, mostly at a trot, then ending with a mad gallop as we tried to head him off, but he escaped into another part of the forest, where the club didn't have the right to hunt.

After the stag escaped, we all gathered around some folding tables that had been set out next to a farmhouse. Wine appeared. My mouth had healed enough that I could drink again, and both Tracy and I were ready for some wine after the long chase. Monsieur le Président sat at one of the tables, across from a man with snow-white hair. We were told that he was a count and that he was crazy. Tracy and I cringed and sank into the background as Monsieur le Président and the crazy count had a screaming argument over what mistakes had been made during the hunt and why the stag had escaped. Often other hunters joined in, but then faded back as the two men continued to fume at each other. Madame from the hotel saw Tracy and me raising eyebrows at each other, but she said, "Don't worry. They are always arguing about something."

And, in fact, when we all met later for dinner at a country inn and sat together at one very long table that had been set up for us, the two men seemed happy and in good humor. The crazy count sat at the head of the table and proceeded to tell jokes—very, very dirty jokes, Madame told us as she laughed along with everyone else at the table. More wine appeared, then the food, then pear eau-de-vie. The crazy count had run out of jokes for the moment and was smiling contentedly, his hands clasped across his stomach. Monsieur le Président stopped by as he was leaving, to pay his respects to Tracy. He was joined by the two other gentlemen who had been in the car. They all made elaborate bows. Tracy was both serene and gracious in the face of all this gallantry in her honor.

That night, in the comfort of our room at the Bas-Bréau, as she lay amid soft pillows on the bed, I made an elaborate bow myself and uttered various polite but long and ornate compliments. Tracy looked puzzled at first, but then smiled indulgently when she realized what I was doing. "Oh, mon cher chéri," she said with her mouth pulled down in a pout, "you have no reason to be jealous of Monsieur le Président."

CHAPTER EIGHT

A Storm During Dinner

Tracy and I went to Paris one more time. We arranged to arrive on May 11, 2005, Tracy's sixty-second birthday. I had just finished writing a book called *The Cave Painters*, which would be published the following year. I never had more fun researching or more difficulty writing than I did while working on that book. The caves I visited were in beautiful areas in rural France, especially around Les Eyzies, in the Périgord, where Vivian and I had seen the statue of the naked caveman. Tracy couldn't come with me during my research, but now I was going to be able to show her some of the things I'd seen. And we would have the means to splurge during the trip. *Gourmet* magazine had commissioned me to write an article on traveling to see the painted caves. The publisher Condé Nast owned *Gourmet*, and, in 2005, expense accounts from Condé Nast were still obscenely lavish.

But we found that extravagance didn't come naturally for us, and we didn't push boundaries by our spending. In Paris, we stayed in a modest but comfortable hotel in the Latin Quarter. After we were settled there, the first thing we did was walk to Georges Thuillier on the Place Saint-Sulpice so Tracy could buy some santons for her birthday. These are small, painted terra-cotta figures that come from various workshops in Provence. The word meant "little saint" in an eighteenth-century Provençal dialect. Santons first appeared during the suppression of the Church and religious services during the French Revolution. Formerly, in the weeks before Christmas in Provence, there were crèches and nativity scenes with living people in costumes playing the traditional roles. They were large public displays. When such religious displays were forbidden, people in Provence began to create small nativity scenes in their homes. But, so as not to upset the authorities, the characters were not the Biblical wise men, shepherds, and Mary and Joseph, but familiar local figures of village life, such as a woodcutter, a fisherman, a fishwife, a butcher, a gardener, a priest, and so on. There were enough different characters so that a whole village could be set up beneath the Christmas tree.

Tracy had discovered santons in a guidebook she read about Provence before a trip we took together to Arles and Aix-en-Provence in 1998. She was enchanted by the story of their origin, and then, when she finally saw them, by the figures themselves. One bright day in Aix, we followed a map on foot down pretty but ghostly quiet streets to the studio and boutique of Santons Fouque, a much-honored workshop for santons that has been run by the same family for four generations. Tracy bought a handful of figures as well as a cliff, a bridge, a stable, and a couple of houses. One of the figures, perhaps her favorite, was a burly painter, who looked somewhat like Cézanne, sitting outdoors before his easel. In time, her collection grew to become a small village.

Each year, not long after Thanksgiving, together with our children and then with our grandchildren, Tracy would spend an afternoon taking the santons out of the boxes where they were carefully stored the rest of the year, wrapped in tissue. Then she would begin to create her village, placing the houses here and there on the small cliff. She made a stream of aluminum foil run down the cliff, and she put a bridge over the stream. Then she placed the figures in groups around the village in a way that suggested that the whole scene had been frozen in one single moment. She also learned how to secrete small lightbulbs throughout the tableau. Children and grandchildren were allowed to look, and perhaps permitted to put one figure carefully where Tracy indicated, but they were sternly warned not ever to touch it at any other time. And then, one night after dinner, with the family around, we turned out all the lights. Tracy lit the hidden bulbs, and the santon village suddenly came alive with a soft glow and mysterious shadows.

No one in Austin had heard of santons, at least no one we knew, so santons became Tracy's special area of expertise, her unique discovery. She even became rather scholarly about them. She belonged to a high-minded town-and-gown organization for women called the Open Forum. Each member in turn had to prepare and present a paper to the club during its monthly meeting. Tracy chose to make a presentation about santons. She gave their history, explained how they were made and painted, and discussed the different qualities of the acknowledged masters of the craft. She described our visit to Santons Fouque and spoke also of Marcel Carbonel of Marseille, who died in 2003 at ninety-one, after decades of dominating both the aesthetics and the marketing of santons. Tracy's paper was a great success with the Open Forum—not a small matter, since they could be a demanding audience. Given confidence, she repeated her talk for our family, for her parents, for my mother, and for anyone else whose interest was piqued by seeing her village in our home during Christmas.

What was it about these figures that so enchanted her? They were French. That was important. Also, certainly, she liked the colors and the forms, as well as the aesthetic pleasure of arranging all the figures in a dramatic and appealing display. And, more than that, I now believe that the santon village was not so removed from Tracy's life before we met as it had always seemed to me before.

When Tracy was growing up in the 1950s, Amarillo was only about seventy years old. It was not a city or even much of a town in those days, but more or less a rural village. It had its stock characters whom everyone knew, such as the grocer, the barber, the haberdasher, the accountant. Of course, there were also other figures—the rancher, the mechanic, the wildcatter. One could almost imagine a crèche surrounded by such small painted terra-cotta figures from life in Amarillo, although that display, with contemporary Texas figures, could only have seemed like a parody. But if, instead, the figures were from two centuries in the past and placed in a rural setting far away from Texas, then sincerity would replace what might have been satire. I believe that with her santons Tracy was creating an imaginary world that was based on her memories of her own life as she was growing up. With them, she could re-create that life as an ideal world of small painted figures around a crèche.

Among such religious objects as medals, rosaries, incense burners, crosses, and icons, Georges Thuillier sells a large selection of santons. Tracy chose a "gitane avec ours"—a Gypsy with a bear—and a chicken coop. The latter was considerably more delicate and charming than it might sound.

It was a bright day. Tracy was radiant in a black leather

jacket, an Hermès scarf, and big, round sunglasses. Despite our sleepless night on the airplane, we were electrified by being back in Paris and ready to walk. Distances didn't matter. From Georges Thuillier, we strolled on to Notre-Dame, where Tracy lit a candle and said a prayer for an elderly neighbor who had died the day before our departure, an artist who had become Tracy's dear friend. We went on to the Île Saint-Louis and, after rambling around for a while, walked across the Pont de la Tournelle to the Left Bank and on to our hotel. It was only six, at least an hour before restaurants began serving, but we found a small Italian café on a quiet square and ate there. "This has been one happy birthday," Tracy said. We drank a carafe of wine and then, back in our room, fell into bed with a weary sigh.

The next morning, more careful about conserving our energy than we had been the day before, we took the Métro to the Louvre and the Palais Royale. But before entering the museum, we went around the corner to the box office of La Comédie Française, on the rue de Richelieu. We bought tickets for *Tartuffe* in eleven days, when we would be back in Paris after our travels across the Dordogne.

We stayed in the Louvre until early afternoon, when we left to have a glass of kir at a café on the square across the rue Saint-Honoré, just south of the Place Colette. As often happened, we said hardly anything but were in constant communication. Under a warm sun, the square was crowded with an ever-changing mass of people of infinite variety. Clothes, attitudes, movements, postures, encounters, embraces, farewells—nothing was really unusual, but everything was both unpredictable and absorbing. Again and again, Tracy and I found ourselves watching the same person at the same time. After a few moments, we would turn to look at each other, eye to eye. By a slight grin, or a barely wrinkled brow, or gentle roll of the eyes, or a barely perceptible downward-turned mouth, we both knew what the other was thinking. Or, more precisely, we both knew that we were thinking exactly the same thing at exactly the same time. I felt these moments of mutual absorption as embraces, and I miss them as much as the physical embraces when we held each other close.

I've had kir on that square several times since that afternoon, most recently just a few weeks before writing this. It's something I try to do at least once each time I visit Paris. The conjunction of the Louvre, La Comédie Française, the Palais Royale, and various popular stores and restaurants still attracts a crowd that offers endless pleasure to an alert observer. I watch and silently consider each person I see. When I feel myself beginning to grin or opening my eyes slightly wider, I feel like Tracy and I are thinking the same thing at the same time, just as we did when we were sitting there together.

. . .

We went on to Les Eyzies the next day, the first leg by train and the second by a rented car. It all began badly. I had always stayed at the Hôtel de France in Les Eyzies and been very comfortable there. It was a short walk downhill to the Café de la Mairie, a pleasant place that was the hub of life in the village. It was run by a married couple with two daughters, all of whom lived above the restaurant. I went there every evening after dinner to order a carafe of wine, write postcards home, and make notes about the research I'd done that day. Since I had been there during the late fall, which was an off season for tourists, I was often the only customer, except for family friends who showed up to have a glass at the bar and watch the soccer match on television with Monsieur. But Tracy took an instant dislike to the Hôtel de France. "You *can't* write about this place for *Gourmet*," she said. She had her reasons. Our room wasn't really ready. There were no towels, no heater, no wastebasket, and she sent me down to the desk to ask for a hair dryer for her. The hotel gladly gave me one. On the way back to the room, I was most grateful that I wasn't going to have to face Tracy empty-handed.

Though she was glad to get the hair dryer, she remained upset. We ignored those storm clouds between us, just as we ignored the dark clouds forming in the sky overhead as we walked to have dinner at the Hôtel Le Cro-Magnon. It was suitably located on the Avenue de la Préhistoire, just a few blocks away, on the edge of town. The Abri Cro-Magnon was just behind the hotel. Here, as I've mentioned, was where the first bones of ancient modern humans, who became known as Cro-Magnon men, were discovered in 1868. The place wasn't much in 2005, just a rock overhang with a plaque and a low rusted fence in front. Now there is a visitors' center, and you have to pay to see the site. The hotel itself abuts a cliff, so entering it felt very much like entering a cave. The restaurant wasn't enclosed at all except for long, clear plastic strips that hung over a frame of iron pipe. The strips shook and even whistled a little with the slightest breeze. By now the sky was covered with thick black clouds, which left the restaurant very dark. We were one of only two couples there.

At the table, Tracy said, "I don't know about all this. You were so happy here before, and now you've got me to please." Just then came a deafening crack of thunder as lightning flashed. For an electric moment, the restaurant lit up as if it were noon.

There was another crack, a sudden strong wind, and heavy raindrops began pelting the plastic ceiling over our heads. In the midst of the storm's fury, the waiter appeared. The heavy rain splattering on the plastic was so loud that we both had to shout for him to hear our orders. Talking was impossible. We sat looking at each other. When the food arrived, it turned out to be better than we had any reason to expect. That dissipated some of the gloom. For dessert we split a nice crème brûlée. Then we drank wine until the rain stopped and we could walk back to the Hôtel de France.

When we opened the door to our room, the first thing we saw was a pile of fresh towels. "Oh, okay," Tracy said. "I'll get off my high horse." She seemed to consider for a moment. "But maybe you don't want me to," she said.

"I don't. I'll get up there with you instead."

"That works," she said, and the clouds that had been gathering between us vanished.

The rest of the trip was idyllic. We visited every cave and archaeological site in the area, which required that we make leisurely drives across the lovely countryside. We ate at the best restaurants in Les Eyzies and in the towns nearby. There were surprisingly many, including one that had two Michelin stars. Late one afternoon, we drove to the motel on the outskirts where Vivian and I had stayed during our ride ten years before. By pure chance or by destiny—I guess it had to be one or the other—Annabelle and the randonnée she was leading were there, turning out their horses into a fenced pasture across the highway from the motel. She remembered Vivian and me and even mentioned the article I'd written. Her husband was there as well. Though he had been remote before, now he was suddenly full of good cheer and laughing, and made a gallant bow when I introduced Tracy.

At one of the caves, we met a prehistorian whom I had known by reputation. She and her artist husband invited us to dinner at their farmhouse outside Les Eyzies. It was large and bright and comfortable. Exquisite art covered the walls, books lay all around, and a savory stew simmered on the stove. As we ate, we could see her husband's graceful, colorful sculptures that he had placed across a meadow and among the trees on the edge of a forest. They had been married almost exactly as long as we had been and had raised their three daughters in this house. They said that they missed having a son, as we had had. I knew that Tracy was comparing their life together in this charming country house in France with ours in Austin, and she knew I was doing the same thing. As we drove back to our hotel, Tracy said, "Maybe in another life." Then she added, "But I'm not complaining. I'm really not. I don't have anything to complain about."

There was a silent moment. "Pretty countryside, though," I said.

"Yes, pretty countryside." There was another silent moment as we looked at the late sun slanting over the winding road. "Maybe in another life," Tracy said again. We had sometimes talked about buying a place in Arles or in Paris, but now we knew we never would. That wasn't sad, particularly. We really didn't have anything to complain about.

·   ·   ·

After ten days, we arrived back in Paris, on a Friday evening, too late for anything but a leisurely dinner near our hotel.

The next morning, we walked across the Luxembourg Gardens. For a while we watched children sailing their toy boats in the pond and then just wandered on into the streets around the park. Our five-year-old granddaughter had asked Tracy to bring her a "standing lion" from Paris. We were both confounded by what this standing lion might be. The granddaughter, certain we would know, couldn't give us any other clues, and there were no lions, standing or otherwise, in the shops we visited.

That evening we went to see *Tartuffe* at La Comédie Française, congratulating ourselves for having had the foresight to have bought our tickets before we set off for the Dordogne. But we were soon to wish we hadn't bothered. Whereas *La Malade imaginaire* had been a delight from beginning to end, this production was an agony to sit through. We were shocked and disappointed. In fact, we felt deceived to see with our own eyes that the productions at La Comédie Française are not dependably good. In this *Tartuffe,* each actor seemed to be doing a solo performance in a private play. There was no love in any love scene. No argument was really an argument, but instead whatever it's called when two individuals shout independently into the void. The costumes were a mélange of styles across the centuries, from doublets to contemporary punk. And we had chosen seats badly as well. The first row of the balcony seemed appealing, but in fact there was a gap of only six inches or so between the seat and the railing, so that we had to sit sideways and couldn't straighten our legs. Looking over the low railing across the audience below us to the stage gave both Tracy and me vertigo. At least it wasn't raining when we finally left the theater.

But the next day, Sunday, our last day in Paris, erased the disappointment of the night before. A breakfast at a farmers' market on the Place Monge, a stroll down to the rue Jacob for a nostalgic return to see the Hôtel d'Angleterre and the Hôtel des Marrionners, lunch at Café de Flore, then across the river to stroll along the Tuileries Gardens, and back across to the Musée d'Orsay so Tracy could see Cézanne's landscapes again, and then along the Seine to visit the Bastille Brocante, a huge garage sale. Tents lined both sides of the river for a mile or more. We looked and looked without buying until we came upon a display of key chains with the Peugeot logo, which is . . . a standing lion. Tracy bought one.

"Could that really be what she meant?" I asked.

Tracy said, "I don't know if it is or isn't, but she asked for a standing lion and she's getting a standing lion."

We had dinner on the rue Mouffetard and walked along afterward, hand in hand, taking our time. The cafés were full of young people and noise and gaiety. I put my arm around Tracy's waist and pulled her close to me and kissed her as we looked into the large open window of a café. A student with curly black hair, his face lit red from wine and excitement, raised his glass to us. Spontaneously, we both blew kisses back toward him. He and his friends all roared and raised their glasses to us in unison.

Slowly, happily, we walked on. "I am filled with Paris," Tracy said suddenly. She was talking both to me and to the whole city around us. "I'm satiated, I'm satisfied, I've done it. At last, I feel like I've done it. I can put my arms around it."

I was happy, too. The trip had given Tracy what she wanted. Now she was focused on getting enough sleep before the airport shuttle arrived at seven-thirty the next morning. That night, sitting on the side of the bed, she wrote a few final words in her journal: "Home to kids, grandkids, and CALVIN!!!!" Calvin was our black cocker spaniel, whom she adored.

Our granddaughter loved her standing lion. That gentle spring evening in 2005 was the last time Tracy saw Paris.

 PART III

The Woman in Saint-Eustache

CHAPTER NINE

Santons and Randonnées

Often, in the weeks and months after her death, in idle moments in my office during the day or while watching my magic DVDs in the evening, I ruminated on the care Tracy had received at MD Anderson. Had those final weeks of painful treatments in Houston, which often left her glum and disoriented, been a big mistake? And what about the hours of driving, and the displacement from our own comfortable home, and her missing the congenial, reassuring company of our children and our friends, all of which made her final weeks lonely and isolated? Had all that effort and all that trouble been worth it? I thought often of that phone call from the cancer survivor, which I never mentioned to her or anyone else. I came to believe that the doctors should have made the very probable futility of her treatments clearer than they did. I even wrote a respectful letter saying so to her principal physician. Our oldest daughter, Liza, says that I shouldn't think that way, that Tracy wanted the treatment no matter what and never wavered from that, even during the hardest days and the darkest hours. She is probably right. I was always going to let Tracy have her way. I had let her have her way throughout our marriage, so why not now?

That's the main reason I kept the phone call to myself. But my unquiet thoughts remained, as well as resentment toward the doctors for making her final days miserable for no very good reason. This remorse and these recriminations are one way my sadness emerged. I felt that sadness as a thudding vibration that penetrated clear through me.

But that was only sadness. I could carry on in spite of it. Real grief arrived as a horrible, ghastly panic that could rise in a single moment, and without warning, from somewhere in the depths within me. I would become hopelessly and helplessly despondent as the waves of grief rolled over me. My stomach contracted painfully, and I thought my head would burst. Sometimes I would call one of our daughters, who were always calm and comforting. But often I didn't want to burden them, and during those times alone I never knew how to mitigate the attacks. I just had to let them run on until I was completely exhausted. A random thought or a song lyric or a phrase in a book would make me erupt in uncontrollable tears. That continued for several years—less frequently as time went on, but with no less intensity when the agony did arrive. I'm sure grief is not through with me yet. It will come again, although I don't know when. Maybe tomorrow, maybe in a year or in five years, but it will come.

When someone in your family is ill, you soon learn to stay clear of well-meaning casual acquaintances. They want to show their concern, so they trap you and ask a series of questions— always the same ones—which you have had to answer time and again with other casual acquaintances in similar situations. Often they want to tell you about an illness that happened to them or to someone in their family, and what the doctor said, and what treatment worked or didn't work, and so on. I was surprised by how many people, always using an urgent but lowered and conspiratorial voice, had wanted to tell me about faith healers. These confidences always began with the same six words—"I know it sounds crazy but"—followed by "there is a man in Brazil who . . ." or "a friend of my sister's went to a woman who . . ."

Such encounters were an annoyance during Tracy's illness, but they went beyond annoyance and led into dangerous territory after her death. Once, I entered the elevator in my building to go down to my car in the garage. Another man was already in the elevator. I didn't know him but I had seen him often enough in the building. He was slender, about my age, and dressed in jeans and a T-shirt, as I was. We rode in silence for a few moments. Then he turned to me and said, "I'm sorry for your loss and your family's loss."

"Thank you."

"She was a beautiful woman. And she was way too young. Way too young."

"Thank you," I said and extended my right hand. "What's your name?"

He shook my hand and told me his name. It meant nothing to me, I didn't know him at all, but suddenly I was overcome with grief. The elevator stopped and the doors opened. I ducked out ahead of him without saying anything. I didn't want him to see me so emotional. When I got into my car, I was heaving, not nauseated but fighting for breath and feeling numb everywhere. He had been trying to be kind. I knew that, but I was still heaving.

Since I couldn't predict when wounds like that would open, I became wary of them and tried to avoid obvious traps or triggers. Even though I sometimes wanted to look through old photo albums, I resisted the temptation. After her death, on January 28, 2011, I began to dread the approach of Tracy's birthday, May 11. Each year, Mother's Day arrived around then, too, sometimes exactly on the 11th.

When those two days arrived in 2011, it had been only a little over three months since I had last seen Tracy in her bed at the hospice. Together, her birthday and Mother's Day combined to form a miserable combination of reminders. On the 11th, I met Liza and Tracy's mother, Shirley, for lunch at a Mexican restaurant. Shirley could be difficult even in ordinary circumstances. Now she was trying to be nice, but it was clear that she had worn on Liza's patience. They had just visited Tracy's grave and planted a small laurel tree. I decided to go visit her grave myself. I had not been there since the funeral. At the cemetery, I had some trouble finding her grave. At one point during my search, I had the strange premonition that the gravestones were going to start spinning, the way the scenery does in a B movie when a character is going insane. But, finally, I did find her grave. In my memory her gravestone was red granite, but in fact it was gray.

A few other visitors were here and there in the cemetery. The closest one, although he was at least forty yards away, was a solitary man about my age. He sat on a bench, staring down at a grave by his feet. Was it his wife's grave? Or maybe a child's? He sat there staring, occasionally taking a deep breath. I thought that we should put a chair or a bench by Tracy's grave. I looked down. Squares of sod made a checkerboard pattern. The squares in the center had sunk slightly below grade. I felt lost again, and turned to go back to my car.

Someone had put a small stone sculpture of the hind legs, rump, and tail of a puppy at one of the nearby graves. It looked as if the puppy had dug far enough into the grave so that his head and the front of his shoulders had disappeared underground. My first thought was that the deceased person had loved dogs, but that thought was immediately swept away by revulsion. The dog was desecrating the grave, searching for bones to chew. The ghastly image of exactly that appeared before my eyes. The dog's mouth was dripping with saliva as it held a human femur in its teeth. I wanted to kick the little sculpture away. I forced myself to keep walking.

I do not believe in ghosts rather more than I believe in them. As a child, I didn't want to sleep with my feet or hands extended over the edge of the mattress, since then the monsters who lived under the bed at night might grab them. Later, when I was fourteen or fifteen, sleeping without a shirt during a summer night before air conditioning, I felt a chill go down my backbone as if a frozen finger had traced a line there. I turned and saw a shade standing by my bed. It was tall, narrow, featureless, as if a robe had been hung on a skeleton. I screamed in terror so loudly that my stepfather, in the bedroom at the end of a hall and behind a closed door, heard me and came rushing through the darkness into my room. He flipped on the light, and, of course, nothing was there.

Now, in the months after Tracy's death, at home in the condominium where we had lived for the last four years of her life—a place so redolent of her, because she had designed a renovation from floor to ceiling and during six months of construction had supervised the contractor so closely that his final bill was under budget by twenty-five cents—I would sometimes find things placed differently from the way I remembered them. Or the thermostat—always a source of minor friction; Tracy liked it cooler than I did—would be lower than I had left it. Tracy drank only bottled water. I bought some to keep in the refrigerator, because, standing there, cool and ready, the bottles reminded me of her. And then, one by one, the bottles began to disappear. I counted. I was certain. I was having a difficult time trying to hold on to the world I knew existed and stay away from the worlds that I believed probably did not exist. Then I figured out that Rosie, the maid, usually drank one of the bottles as she worked. She was the explanation for the changed thermostat as well.

Then, one night, around three, I heard a beeping. I knew it was our refrigerator. It beeps if it has been left open. There are two doors, side by side. If you are not careful, it's easy to pop one door open when you close the other one. I got out of bed and walked the length of the apartment to the kitchen in the dark. When I turned on the light in the kitchen, I saw that, indeed, the left-side door was ajar. I pushed it closed, careful not to force the right door open, and the beeping stopped. But then I wondered, "Why did it start beeping now?" It usually started just a few moments after it had been left open, but I had been asleep for hours. With no easy answer to the question, I turned out the kitchen light and went back to bed.

A few minutes later, I heard the beeping again. I walked through the dark to the kitchen a second time. Now the right-side door was open. That couldn't be—I had made sure both sides were shut. But, groggy with sleep, maybe I had made a mistake. I pushed the door closed, and the beeping stopped. I returned to bed.

Before long, the beeping started again. Now I was frightened. The sharp, insistent sound, repeating every five seconds in the quiet of the night, was a horrifying torture. I did not want to go back into the kitchen. The beeps continued relentlessly, one and another and another and another. I had to stop them. I turned on the light in the bedroom. I opened the door and flipped the switch so the hallway lights came on. I stepped into the hallway. Nothing was there. I stepped over to the switch that turned on the lights in the living room. My cat looked at me quizzically from the chair where she was sleeping. I went to the kitchen and turned on the light. There was nothing there. I was breathing heavily. Both refrigerator doors were closed, but the beeping continued. I opened the doors and closed them again. The beeping never faltered. I opened the doors again. The bottles and packages inside were all sweating. The refrigerator was beeping because the internal temperature was higher than it should have been. Tracy and I had confronted this a couple of times before and could never figure out how to make the beeping stop. We just closed the doors and waited.

Back in bed, even with the bedroom door closed, I could hear the relentless beeping. I couldn't stop listening for it. I felt mocked and silly for being frightened, but I *was* frightened. Was there really nothing there? Evidently not. In the morning, everything was normal. As I stood in front of the refrigerator, my cat rubbed against my ankles and rolled over on her back

A few nights later, I had a terrible dream and woke up tossing and screaming, to discover several other people hiding in the bed with Tracy and me. We were all lying in a row, as stiff as boards, seeking safety together from some merciless, revolting, oozing plasma. Then I woke up for real and realized that I had only dreamed of waking up. I was alone in my own bed with the covers in a wad beside me.

Now, years later, I don't always dream, but when I do, Tracy is often in the dream. I haven't called to her, nor does she materialize as if she had come from another world. She is simply there, and in my dreams she is always alive. That seems perfectly normal in the dream, although nothing ever happens between us. I think of these dreams as visitations. When I awaken, I'm disappointed and feel empty.

.   .   .

After the difficulties I had in 2011, during the weeks around Tracy's birthday and Mother's Day, I knew I would need some agreeable distraction to carry me up to, through, and beyond May 11 in 2012. I had no trouble deciding what that distraction would be. I would take another randonnée à cheval in France.

But I had quit riding in 2002, bored with the way I was riding. To improve and move forward, I would have had to buy and maintain a good horse and spend a lot more time in the saddle. I decided that wasn't the way I wanted to spend my money or my time. Now, in 2012, I hadn't been on a horse in ten years. I went back to the stables where I had begun, and rode in the ring twice a week. The riding master was a funny, intelligent, and strict woman who called out sloppy riding or bad habits mercilessly. With her help, it didn't take me long to find my leg again, especially since I felt comfortable in the saddle almost immediately. Part of that comfort came from feeling a pleasant and unexpected connection with Tracy as I remembered our times together at this stable, and at horse shows with our daughter. But I didn't take any fences. There wouldn't be jumping on the ride I was planning, and I didn't want even a slight amount of added risk. I pulled my horse to the side and watched as the other riders ran through courses taking multiple fences, turning corners, and effortlessly changing leads. Once, I could have done all that myself, but those days were behind me now.

Watching the other riders taking a difficult course of fences, I always felt a little frisson of mortality.

I made a reservation for a ride across the Dordogne, which I chose because it began before and ended after May 11, 2012. I stopped in Paris for a few days in late April, so I could get over jet lag before the ride began. I took a small—very small—room in a small—very small—hotel on the rue Victor-Cousin, near the Sorbonne and the Panthéon. I chose that hotel in part because it looked reasonably nice and wasn't expensive, but mostly because Tracy and I had never stayed there or in that neighborhood. I liked it immediately, and took pleasure in thinking that she would have liked it, too.

The rue Victor-Cousin intersects the broad rue Soufflot, which runs from the Boulevard Saint-Michel to the Place du Panthéon. It's very stately and lined with appealing cafés and restaurants. But the side streets in the neighborhood are narrow and often twist around one another. There are many bookstores, small academic presses, and art-movie theaters. In the Place de la Sorbonne, at the foot of the rue Victor-Cousin, there are cafés crowded with animated students, and there are interesting shops everywhere and a couple of cavernous used-book stores. Surely, they held the wisdom of the ages if only you could find it among the almost petrified stacks of ancient volumes.

I gladly returned to the Louvre, the Musée d'Orsay, and other obligatory stops that Tracy and I had always made together, but I found I liked wandering around this new neighborhood just as much. I actually said "Aha!" out loud when I turned a corner and discovered a magic shop. (Since then, in the manner of many magic shops these days, it has disappeared.)

Tracy and I had discovered a Paris together that we both loved. But now, during odd moments as I wandered, I began to think that there might also be much more in Paris that was there waiting for me, a Paris filled with wonders and mysteries and pleasures that I could discover without betraying or abandoning either Tracy or the Paris that we had found together.

The ride was splendid, and it did for me emotionally what I had hoped that it would. Unfortunately, the only other rider was a woman from South Africa who was inane and proudly wealthy, a deadly combination. She was riding while her husband followed the pilgrimage to Santiago de Compostela. While we were on horseback, I was usually able to ignore her, although meals were another matter. We began riding on a Sunday morning and ended on a Friday evening, but after the first day I lost—or, rather, fled from—all sense of time. The eleventh day of May came and went without my knowing when.

Jean, the outfitter, was a tall, lanky horseman about forty who wore jeans and pearl-snap shirts and looked as much like a cowboy as any Frenchman could look. In his van he had a score of country music CDs. Béatrice, his assistant, was a tiny woman with short white hair. She drove a separate van with our luggage. Each day, she went ahead to the place where we would stop for lunch outdoors and had the food and wine ready when we arrived. The lunches always took about two hours. This was partly to rest the horses, but, then, Jean wasn't in any hurry, either. I had to make myself slow down in order to enjoy such a leisurely lunch. My solution, after eating and drinking several glasses, was to find a comfortable spot and lie in the sun with a hat over my eyes. That way, I got a little rest and also avoided the woman from South Africa.

After lunch, Béatrice drove on to that night's hotel, so our luggage was there when we arrived. The South African woman and I remounted and followed Jean for the afternoon. It was real riding, with frequent long gallops across the countryside during which the only sound was the horses' hooves pounding the ground. Then, as we walked, mounted, through villages, the clanging of the horseshoes on stone streets excited a frenzied barking by the local dogs. The villages hadn't changed much over the years, and I had the feeling of going back in time, way back long before the automobile or the train. The trip was expensive, but the hotels were always comfortable, and the evening meals were elegant feasts with very fine local wine, which made up for having to dine with Lady South Africa. So, for six days, the only decision I had to make was which shirt to put on in the morning. I had not a single worry, because I knew that the next day would follow the same pattern as the one that had just ended. And one chance moment confirmed for me that this ride had been a fortunate choice that had been meant for me all along.

A few years earlier, I had somehow lost the Nontron knife that Tracy had given me before the stag hunt. I think I must have left it in a hotel room. During the days in Paris before this randonnée, I had gone back to the rue de Richelieu to buy another Nontron knife, only to find that the elegant store with hunting equipment near La Comédie Française had closed. That was a disappointment. But one evening during the ride, while wandering around before dinner in the little town where we had stopped for the night, I found a cutlery store. It seemed odd to me to find a pricy specialty store in such a small village. I entered out of curiosity, and immediately saw a large display of Nontron knives, including the same model of pocket knife that Tracy had given me. I bought one to replace the one I had lost.

I use it constantly at home and always bring it with me when I travel.

I lingered in Paris for a few days after the ride had ended. I could no longer forget, and didn't want to forget, that Tracy's birthday had come and gone just a few days ago. I had bought the Nontron knife as if it were a present from her to me. Now, in Paris, I wanted to buy a present from me to her. I knew that I wanted to give her some santons, and I knew I could find them in Georges Thuillier, on the Place Saint-Sulpice.

I spent a long time choosing among the many santons for sale before deciding on a woman wearing a traditional red dress from Arles and a woman carrying a basket of bread. I chose the Arlésienne because Tracy and I were enthralled with Arles when we visited there in 1998. We stayed at the Grand Hôtel Nord-Pinus, with the dramatic statue of the Provençal poet Frédéric Mistral (Nobel Prize, 1904) in front, and the restaurant where van Gogh painted *The Night Café* just to the side. Photographs of Africa by Peter Beard enhance the bar. In one taken with a powerful flash at night, a beautiful nude woman is feeding a leaf to a giraffe. After some wine, Tracy stood by our table and parodied the pose while feeding me a peanut. I chose the woman carrying a basket of bread not because Tracy baked bread—she didn't, although she cooked divinely—but because that santon seemed to represent generosity and hospitality.

The statues were about three inches tall. The cashier in Georges Thuillier wrapped them in tissue and then put them in a stiff cardboard box, which kept them safe in my suitcase during my flight home. The day after my arrival, I drove to the cemetery and put the two figures on the base of Tracy's tombstone. Even today, they still valiantly keep watch over her in the summer heat or the wet winter cold. By now, they are worn slightly, but not as much as you would expect after more than eight years exposed to the elements.

.   .   .

I rode with Jean again during early May the following year, 2013. Once again, we crossed beautiful country, stayed in comfortable hotels, and were served splendid dinners. This time, there were four other riders, all of them agreeable company. During the day, it was pleasant being outdoors on horseback beneath a gentle sun, following along behind Jean. With little else to occupy my mind, I sometimes found myself pondering my situation and wondering what I should do.

I didn't want to spend the rest of my evenings drinking alone and watching magic DVDs, comforting as that had been for the past two years. When I thought about romance, which I did less often than I would have thought, I knew that I would like to find another woman and be in love again, but I made only a few faint efforts to find someone. I encountered one or two women for whom I had some hopes, but when I asked them out, I was refused evasively. I found those moments, standing in front of a woman who was looking to the side while she searched for a polite way to say no to me, more painful than they should have been. I wasn't ready emotionally for even the slightest rejection.

Eighteen months after Tracy's death, I did have one romance that began well enough, but then fizzled when I backed away. "You aren't over Tracy," the woman said. "I never had a chance." And she was right.

In my solitude after Tracy's death, I had made three resolutions about women. I would not become involved with anyone who had children still at home, or anyone who smoked, or anyone who had cancer. I was sixty-six when Tracy died. I had enjoyed having a young family once, but I didn't want another one now. I had come to hate cigarette smoke and the smell of tobacco on the clothes and in the hair of smokers. And I had watched Tracy lose her battle with cancer and didn't want to suffer through that experience again.

But, shortly after making those resolutions, I was invited to a fancy horse show in Houston. There was an attractive woman in a vermillion sheath at the next table. She wasn't wearing a wedding ring and wasn't there with a man. She didn't seem to have cancer and she wasn't smoking, but she did have two young daughters. The girls looked to be around six and eight. They wore pretty ruffled dresses, and their mother had obviously scrubbed their faces and carefully brushed and combed their hair. And they were very polite and perfectly behaved without being stiff. I asked the older one if she rode horseback over fences.

"Yes," she said.

"Are you scared?"

"No," she said solemnly. "You have to trust your horse and you have to trust yourself."

I found all this so charming that a few moments later I whispered to my host, "Do you know that woman at the next table?"

"Yes."

"Is she married?"

"Yes," he said.

"She's not wearing a ring."

He looked over. "No, I guess not, but she's married."

"Okay," I said. "Never mind."

During the rest of the evening, I looked their way from

time to time. The girls were enjoying themselves but always charming. The woman was gay and happy. Despite my promise to myself about avoiding women with children at home, I started imagining a life together with this woman and her two young daughters. Evidently, at least one of my resolutions was more flexible than I thought.

Not that my newly acknowledged flexibility made much difference. I never had a date. After those early one or two refusals, there was no one I knew in Austin whom I wanted to ask out. I didn't know anything to do but just wait for someone to come along. When I tried the Internet, I found that looking for dates there took a vast amount of time for meager results. I was surprised to receive two different elliptical phone calls from married women whom I vaguely knew. They were both well outside even my extended circle of friends. I played dumb and gave cues so they could back away and get off the phone naturally, while we both pretended not to notice any undercurrent in our brief conversation.

I had not been especially tempted, but those calls prompted another resolution, which was not flexible, even if a more tempting situation were to occur. I wanted neither deceit nor messy complications. Why introduce tension and lies and clandestine meetings and fear of discovery into my life? I kept thinking that at the university, where there was a faculty and staff of about ten thousand people, there must be a woman somewhere who would be right for me, and probably somewhere there was. But, except for some aspects of undergraduate life, the university isn't a social club. There isn't much mixing among the academic departments. The ideal woman in, say, the College of Natural Sciences is someone I, teaching in the College of Liberal Arts and working at the Ransom Center, would never meet.

CHAPTER TEN

A Visitation

At the end of my 2013 ride, after saying goodbye to Jean and the other riders, I lingered for a few days in Paris. I made my pilgrimage to Georges Thuillier, where I bought a somewhat larger santon of an Arlésienne to stand watch on the other side of Tracy's tombstone. I had been given the names of a young couple who were friends of a friend. I hadn't thought I would use that connection, since I knew they were at least thirty years younger than I was, but one morning, on a whim, I called anyway. That random, offhand call changed the course of my life.

The young woman was French, her husband was American, and they had a daughter who was eighteen months old. We spent considerable time together in the few days remaining for me in Paris. I think I was a welcome distraction for them from a rather difficult time they were having, living in Paris with a toddler, adorable as she was. For one thing, their apartment was on the fifth floor of a building with no elevator, a difficult climb under any circumstances but especially demanding while carrying a squirming child.

One evening, tired from a few long promenades across

the Luxembourg Gardens, we were sitting in their apartment, gazing idly out the tall casement windows, while twilight fell. The little girl occupied herself by moving toys from one small pile on the parquet floor to another small pile, and then moving them back. The young father, in the midst of talking about something else, mentioned casually that he was learning French in classes at the Sorbonne in a course called French Language and Civilization that was specifically for foreigners. I suddenly came to life. "Can *anyone* take the course?" I asked. "Could *I* take that course?" That was the first of many questions that rapidly followed. I saw a world of new possibilities opening before me. I was immediately certain that I could learn French in Paris at the Sorbonne. And I would be living in Paris all the while I was attending classes. I would drown myself in the language and the culture. I would mix with French people easily, I would order with assurance in a café, I would go to poetry slams and laugh with everyone else at the jokes, I would listen to jazz at a bar and talk about the music with the bartender while the band took a break, I would attend learned lectures on the history of art at the Louvre, I would hear classical concerts in the churches, I would walk into a bookstore and know the best new novels. All this and more ran through my mind as images, not as thoughts: I saw myself at the café, at the bar, at the concert, and at the lecture.

My new young friend showed me the course's Web site. It certainly looked serious, a full college curriculum that had spring, summer, and fall semesters. The students were in class twenty hours a week. In addition to the grammar classes, there were lectures on French literature, French art, French film, and so on. All this intensified my reveries. I was enraptured. It was all real, and not just a dream. I could make it happen. I began talking about registering for the spring 2014 semester, which would start next January and last well into May.

Back in Austin, I began the process of getting admitted to the course. The online application was detailed and created some absurd moments. I would be sixty-nine in January 2014. The application asked for the year of the student's birth; it had a scroll that started at 2000 and went back from there. But the numbers stopped at 1965, long before 1944, when I was born. I didn't know what else to do except enter the oldest year on the scroll. With a single click, I sliced more than twenty years off my age. The only prerequisites for the course were a deposit, proof that you had enough money to pay the surprisingly reasonable tuition and to support yourself while in Paris, a student visa, and a copy of your high-school diploma. That made me laugh. The high school I attended had been shuttered for more than twenty years. It would be impossible to get a copy of my records, which had probably disappeared long ago anyway. My hard-earned diploma from Rice University would have to do.

I had to go to the French Consulate in Houston to apply for a student visa. As required, I took bank statements showing that I had enough money to support myself while I was in Paris. I was interviewed by a man who sat behind a bulletproof glass window. He did indeed want to see my bank statements, which I slid through a small crack at the bottom of the window. Since he nodded and made a note or two before sliding them back through the crack, I assumed the question of money was settled. But he was skeptical when he saw my age, and confused that, even though I worked and taught at the University of Texas, I was applying for a student visa. "Which are *you?*" he asked. "A stu*dent?* A pro*fesseur?*" In the end, however, he was friendly and even expedited a few small details. With my student visa, I could stay in France legally for six months.

I found an apartment through a Web site intended for professors on sabbatical leave. My prospective landlord, an American historian whose French wife studied nineteenth-century American literature, knew Austin because he had taught at the University of Texas for a semester several years earlier. During a phone call, we discovered the extraordinary coincidence that, during their time in Austin, he and his wife had rented the apartment of a friend of mine who lives in the same building as I do, on the floor above me.

And so, on a sunny but cold day in mid-January 2014, I found myself pulling a suitcase with one hand and a stuffed duffel bag with the other down the Boulevard de Port-Royal toward my rented apartment. I had managed to find the train from Charles de Gaulle Airport and had gotten off at the correct stop. Was being a Parisian really going to be this easy and this pleasant?

.   .   .

My apartment was in a complex of three-story buildings that had been built in the early 1900s as housing for workers at the nearby fabric factories known as Les Gobelins. There was a black metal gate across the entrance on the Boulevard de Port-Royal, but my landlord had given me the code, which I punched into the electronic box; with a slight buzz, the gate opened. I got the key to the apartment from the guardian, then walked about thirty yards down a cobblestone drive to a second door, where I punched in a second code. Inside, I climbed a wooden spiral staircase with an appealing curved handrail to the second floor. My apartment was to the right, at the end of a short hallway, behind a heavy blue door. It had a brass handle, not on the side near the lock, but right in the middle.

Inside, the apartment was perhaps a little severe, but comfortable nonetheless. A narrow entry hallway ended in a large living room. To the right, a doorway led to a small, open kitchen. Behind it, another doorway led to the bathroom. To the left, yet another doorway led to the bedroom, which had a double bed and an armoire with sliding mirrored doors. There were bare parquet floors throughout, except in the bathroom, which was tiled. Five tall casement windows—three facing west and two facing east—let in plenty of light. The white walls were bare, but there were two bookcases, which held a small but interesting collection of early editions of nineteenth-century American women writers, including *The Minister's Wooing* by Harriet Beecher Stowe and *The Poems of Celia Thaxter*. There was history, too, represented by Louis Blanc's *Histoire de la Révolution française* in twelve volumes, published in Paris in 1862, and M. A. Thiers's *Histoire du consulat et de L'empire* in twenty volumes, also published in Paris in 1862, in concert with Blanc's history of the Revolution. That made thirty-two volumes covering about thirty-two years of French history. During my stay, I sometimes thumbed through them, thinking that it would be a marvelous thing to have read them all but knowing that I never would. There were also some excellent books of photography—Man Ray, Eugène Atget, Gary Winogrand—and helpful histories of Paris, including Jacques Hillairet's two-volume *Dictionnaire historique des rues de Paris*, a classic that tells the history of every street in Paris. In some cases the history is just a line or two, but more often the entries are detailed, run along for several pages, and are illustrated with archival photographs and drawings. In the following months, as I improved at reading French, I spent several evenings mentally wandering through time on the streets of Paris with one or the other of these heavy volumes on my lap.

After I had looked all around the apartment, which took three minutes at the very most, I sat down at a glass table about a yard square; during my stay, it would be my breakfast table, my lunch table, my dinner table, and my desk. It was by one of the casement windows that looked out over a small garden. Before I unpacked my bags, I wanted to feel what it was like to be here in this apartment in Paris. But as I sat there, looking around me, all I could do was wonder what deft touches Tracy would have added to make the place more appealing. With the subtraction of a few small things and the addition of a few different small things, she could make any room come to life. After my stepfather, Bill Curtis, died, my mother moved into an apartment designed for aging in place. She was lamenting one afternoon while we were there that her living room just wasn't right. She was going to hire a decorator, but Tracy said, "Vivian, all you need to do is rearrange your furniture." She put my brother and me to work, moving things around, and that alone transformed the apartment to my mother's great delight. I tried to look at the Paris apartment the way Tracy would have, and to imagine what possibilities she might see, but I failed utterly. She was the one with an eye.

The apartment was on the northern border of the Thirteenth Arrondissement, a quiet corner of Paris where, I would learn, there is much of interest, but not a single tourist destination. It's a neighborhood of families, and of older people who remained there after their children had grown and moved away.

I felt a kinship with them, since my own children were grown and on their own. I liked going out just before dusk, when solitary men and women appeared on the sidewalks to walk their dogs. These beloved pets were surprisingly well behaved, not barking or pulling on the leash. More than a few followed along without any leash at all. Very often these dogs were old, like their masters. With their stiff backs and stiff legs, the dogs looked like tables walking.

Near me there were several cafés, an antiques store, a tailor, a small bookstore run by a sweet woman whose friends stopped by in the afternoon to gossip with her, a second bookstore, devoted entirely to travel writing, and an excellent bakery where I treated myself occasionally to a pain aux raisins. There was another bakery, not quite as good, only half a block farther away. There were two cafés on the corner nearby. One, the Val Café, was filled each night with students drinking beer and smoking cigarettes; catty-corner, in the Lilou, an older crowd silently sipped coffee or wine.

In addition to several Asian take-out places, there were also four very fine restaurants. The Florina was right next door. It was open only for dinner, offering two or three original and inventive dishes. The two chefs started working in the early afternoon. I would often see them standing on the sidewalk, taking a break to smoke a cigarette. (How can it be that chefs, who make their living by producing dishes with superb taste, are so often smokers?) The Languedoc, directly across the street, was a family-run restaurant that has been there since 1974. Very comfortable and homey, it was a sort of clubhouse for the longtime residents of the neighborhood. Madame cooks, and Monsieur, who is the son of the founders, waits tables. The

Languedoc served traditional southwestern French cuisine, very well prepared and without any contemporary frills at all. It was one of two restaurants where I liked to take friends who visited Paris while I was there.

The other restaurant was Le Petit Pascal. Just down the block from my apartment but on the rue Pascal, which runs under the Boulevard de Port-Royal, this tiny restaurant had the charm of being a place you could never find on your own. The garrulous owner of the shop where I bought wine was the one who told me about it. Le Petit Pascal had stone-and-mortar walls, plain wooden tables, wicker chairs, and no other décor whatsoever. Yet it was warm and inviting. Two older women and a much younger one, perhaps a daughter, cooked and waited tables. I learned just to order that night's special, no matter what it was, and that never failed. And the fourth restaurant, OKA, just a block away to the north, had a window on the street that looked into the kitchen, where three or four chefs worked feverishly all afternoon. OKA was very simply decorated, even austere, and may have been the best of the four, but it was so expensive that I never ate there.

In fact, I don't enjoy eating in a restaurant by myself, so most nights I chose among a handful of options for takeout. I learned to avoid the Asian places. They are so popular that they are everywhere all across Paris. Perhaps I never found just the right one, but the food, which always looked so good to me in the window, inevitably disappointed me when I got home. Instead, I shopped at the large farmers' market just across the boulevard from my apartment on Tuesdays, Thursdays, and Saturdays. There, among much else, I could buy paella, ham and sausage with sauerkraut, tomatoes farcis, endive stuffed

with ham in a cream sauce, and a perfect homemade lasagna.
And just a five-minute walk away, Le Relais Gourmet offered
slightly more expensive but carefully crafted cuisine—coq
au vin, for example, or more adventurous dishes they created
themselves.

. . .

Registration for classes came a few days after my arrival.
I was lucky that my apartment was not far from the Boulevard
Raspail, where the school was located. I could get there easily
in twenty minutes or so by walking west along the Boulevard
de Port-Royal to the Boulevard Raspail. There was also a convenient bus, which I took when it was raining, but otherwise I
preferred to walk, for the exercise and to see what was going on
in the neighborhood. A short way west of my apartment was a
fire station where the firemen—"pompiers"—frequently laid
out long hoses to dry on the sidewalk. Several times, I saw a
troop of ten or twelve emerge in formation, wearing identical
jerseys, shorts, and running shoes. They took off jogging down
the sidewalk at a rapid pace. A little farther on, I passed a large
hospital complex on the south side of the boulevard and, on the
north side, a military hospital set back from the street. Double
rolls of concertina barbed wire coiled all around the perimeter
of the large lawn. Neighboring the military hospital was the
Church of the Val-de-Grâce and its elegant dome. In the 1620s,
it was a retreat for Queen Anne of Austria, mother of Louis
XIV, whose heart was once preserved in the chapel. Then,
rebuilt from plans by the architect François Mansart, it became
by turns a convent, a hospice for unwed mothers and found-
lings, a military hospital, and finally, today, a surgical hospital
administered and staffed by the military. At night, illuminated

all around, the ghostly, pale dome rises in splendid isolation against the darkness.

As it crosses the Boulevard Saint-Michel, the Boulevard de Port-Royal changes its name to become the famous Boulevard du Montparnasse. At this intersection, partially hidden behind thick foliage, is La Closerie de Lilas, a bar and restaurant that Hemingway patronized in the 1920s, when he lived above a sawmill just around the corner. The sawmill is long gone, but La Closerie de Lilas remains popular today.

Just outside La Closerie stands the statue of Marshal Ney, with his sword raised high in his right hand. The names of the sixty or so battles in which he fought are carved in the plinth. Hemingway mentions this statue in *A Moveable Feast*. Napoleon called Ney, who fought with him in Russia and also at Waterloo, "the bravest of the brave." Ney was convicted of treason by the restored monarchy in 1815 and executed by a firing squad on the Avenue de l'Observatoire on December 7, at a spot not far from where his statue stands today. Ney refused a blindfold and insisted that he himself give the order for the soldiers to fire.

In 1868, the Academic artist Jean-Léon Gérôme painted an imagined version of Ney's execution. On a dark, damp day, the body of Marshal Ney lies facedown in a muddy road in front of a bare wall as the firing squad marches away into the mist. The painting was criticized in its day, but I find it affecting. You can see the Paris Observatory in the background, behind the wall where the execution took place, as you can see the observatory today from the site of Ney's statue. His first name was Michel, and Hemingway refers to him as "Mike." Ney had abundant, curly red hair, and his men, who loved him, called him Le Rougeaud, or the Red, so perhaps Hemingway wasn't presumptuous to be so familiar. I grew fond of the statue myself and accorded it a certain respect. In the coming months, I would look for it each time I walked by on my way to or from school. If Napoleon said a man was brave, he was brave.

In 1818, someone calling himself Peter Stuart Ney arrived by sailing ship at Charleston, South Carolina. He became a wandering schoolteacher and in the 1840s moved to Davidson, North Carolina, home of the newly founded Davidson College. He designed a seal for the college that is still used today. Peter Stuart Ney had extensive knowledge of Napoleon's campaigns and was said to have been much affected by the news of Napoleon's death in 1821. On his own deathbed in 1846 Peter Stuart Ney claimed to his doctor that he was in fact Marshal Michel Ney, that his execution had been faked, and that he had escaped with the help of some of his former comrades in Napoleon's army who were Freemasons, like himself. The story gained believers. Over the years, a number of articles and books that seemed to be well researched were published. Some contained accounts from former soldiers in Napoleon's army who claimed to have seen Peter Stuart Ney in the Carolinas and had recognized him as the real Marshal Michel Ney. The Davidson library holds a rather large archive of papers and publications concerning this historical "mystery." However, in the 1950s, a man named William Henry Hoyt found various documents in France that described Ney's execution in detail and contained verified proof that the corpse that lay on the ground in front of the firing squad was that of Marshal Michel Ney.

So Peter Stuart Ney's story was a hoax after all. He was a precursor to later frauds, such as Brushy Bill Roberts of Hico, Texas, who claimed to be Billy the Kid in the years before he died in 1950. Or J. Frank Dalton of Granbury, Texas, who died in 1951, claiming he was Jesse James. Or the various men and women over the years who have claimed to be surviving members of Russia's royal Romanov family who had escaped execution by the Bolsheviks in 1918. I mention all this because, while living in Paris, especially during my first stay, in 2014, I have sometimes felt like an impostor myself, as if I had simply disappeared from my former life and reappeared in Paris under the same name but as a different person who is leading a different life and does not have a past. That I knew no one in Paris, and that I spoke French and not English with the people I encountered, only intensified this feeling of deception, if deception is what it was. Perhaps Peter Stuart Ney, having moved to a different country, where he had to speak a different language, invented his story because he had similar feelings of having a new but isolated life without any past. He had never tried to profit from his story during his lifetime. He revealed it only as he was dying, perhaps to give his anonymous life without any past some meaning.

Once the Boulevard de Port-Royal changes to the Boulevard du Montparnasse, it becomes more interesting. There are restaurants of various kinds that in the evenings seemed to do a steady but modest business, except for two cafés not far apart that were always completely filled, every seat at every table taken, and no one there over twenty-five. There is the very intellectual bookshop Tschann, which dates to 1929, which was just after Hemingway's era: he lived in Paris from 1921 to 1928. One day in Tschann I saw a translation of Larry McMurtry's *Duane's Depressed*, one of his finest novels, with the title *Duane est dépressif.* Nearby is a noodle house where, through a window, I could see the immense, fat, almost perfectly round Chinese chef standing by a heavy wooden table where he repeatedly pulled and folded noodle dough in a bliz-

zard of white flour that he sprinkled on the wooden table, the
dough, and everywhere else. Farther west along the Boulevard
du Montparnasse are La Coupole, Le Dôme, and La Rotonde,
more reminders of Hemingway's Paris. La Coupole still looks
elegant, and it's not a bad place for a glass of wine in the afternoon. But it has become notorious as a place where young men
go to attach themselves to older women.

At Le Dôme, which remains an appealing establishment,
the Boulevard du Montparnasse is intersected by the Boulevard
Raspail. I turned left here. The school was just thirty yards or
so south. There was a kiosk on this corner, where I stopped
each day to look at the headlines and the magazine covers. The
man who ran it was a popular neighborhood character. He had
various cronies. I would see him surrounded by some business-
men in suits and the route man who delivered the piles of newspapers. They arrived armed with jokes, which they told each
other under their breath, then bursting into laughter. When
elderly widows arrived to buy their *Le Monde* or *Paris Match*,
he would come out from behind his counter to kiss them on
the cheek and pay extravagant compliments on their dress or
their hair.

At the school, I had a preliminary interview with a woman
who just wanted to be sure I had my visa, my certificate of preregistration, and the means to pay the tuition. I showed her my
passport and—once again—my most recent bank statement.
Then I was told to sit in a white plastic chair at the end of a row
of identical chairs, all occupied by registering students. This
row turned out to snake around the edges of two rooms, so
there were perhaps fifty chairs in all. When someone was called
from the end of the row, everyone moved down one chair.
Meanwhile, as we waited, everyone, including me, was eye-

ing everyone else, all of whom were presumably in the course. There were probably twice as many women as men. Although some of the students might have been as young as eighteen, the majority seemed to be in their early twenties. And then there was a sprinkling of older oddities, like me. I later found out that there were about seven thousand students at the school.

I kept moving down the chairs one by one until it was my turn. The nice young woman sitting behind a desk asked if I wanted to speak French or English. I said English. "So you're sure you understand," she said, and I said yes. She checked my visa, verified my preregistration, and then ran my credit card to pay the tuition. At 1,880 euros, around $2,500, it was not especially expensive for twenty hours of instruction a week for four months. She took my photo, and in a few seconds handed me an official Sorbonne student ID.

Now it was time for the tests that would determine what class I would be put in. Along with fifty or sixty others, I was ushered into two adjoining classrooms and handed a test by a very efficient, almost severe woman. All her instructions were in French, and I was a little unclear how long this test would take. The first page had sentences with blanks to be filled in by a verb in the proper tense. The questions were increasingly difficult, and a few I didn't understand at all. When I came to those parts of the test, I had no idea what question they were asking or what answer they were looking for. Then there was a paragraph in French to read, followed by questions. This was not too difficult, since, as in similar tests in the United States, the questions are in the order in which the answers appear in the text. The crafty student soon learns to read the questions first, then skim through the text to find the answers. Then we listened to a recording twice and had to answer six questions on what we had just heard. I had not understood the recording at all. I just guessed on the questions. I'm sure I missed them all. On the last page of the test, we were asked to write about a sport we participate in. I wrote about riding horses. Then we took our tests and formed another line, waiting for our private interviews. I had a sweet middle-aged woman who asked me why I was taking the course. I said that learning French had been a dream all my life. Also, I wrote books that often required research in French. She asked about my books, and then where I lived. She told me that in a few days I'd get an e-mail with my schedule, and that was that. I was home by two-fifteen. I left feeling as if the round Chinese chef had been pulling and folding my brain. In fact, I'm certain now that I did even worse than I might have imagined. The first classes would begin two weeks later. During the interim, the school would grade the tests, determine each student's level, and constitute the classes.

I had two weeks to kill. I didn't know anyone, so they were two weeks to kill alone. I supposed that I would revisit the famous museums, but I decided to save that for later. The next day was bright and clear, and I set out to find the Arènes de Lutèce, a Roman coliseum that, improbable as this seems, is still preserved in the middle of Paris. I found the Arènes on the blue-and-yellow Michelin map that I had bought almost twenty-two years before, on my first visit to Paris with Tracy.

I walked north up the rue Monge, looking for a hotel near the Place Monge where Tracy and I had stayed during our last trip to Paris together, in 2005. I couldn't remember the name, but I was certain that I would know it if I saw it. And I did. It was the Hôtel Saint Christophe on the corner of the rue Monge and the rue Lacépède. We had stayed there because it was in a part of Paris we had never seen. It was early spring, and we slept with the windows open. There was some noise from the street, but we made a pact not to let it bother us, and it didn't.

How was it that we didn't find the Arènes on that trip? The amphitheater is in a large park just a block north of the hotel. We must have always gone in other directions. Though we nearly always left with a purpose and seldom spent long wandering, one afternoon, while she was resting, I did go north over a slight hill and found a record store across the street from the park, but I didn't venture farther. It was the best jazz record shop I'd ever been in. I told Tracy how hard it had been not to buy anything. We didn't have room in our luggage.

The Arènes was built in the first century and abandoned in the fourth. After that, it became a cemetery and was completely filled in when an adjacent fortified wall was built, about 1200. The amphitheater was rediscovered only in 1869, when Baron Haussmann was cutting a swath through the neighborhood, destroying any building in his way, to create the rue Monge. The Paris Municipal Council, which had become annoyed that this ancient structure was in the way of development, would have destroyed the Arènes, except for an impassioned letter that Victor Hugo wrote in 1883.

The round floor is surrounded by rising rows of stones laid as seats. Below the grandstands are large cages that held wild beasts that were released for the gladiators to fight. Sometimes the spectators watched as a condemned man was executed by being turned out into the arena with ferocious animals that had not been fed for several days. The arena was large enough for seventeen thousand spectators to witness the spectacle. Plays were performed there as well, during which benches were brought onto the floor. A canopy supported by cables protected at least some of the amphitheater from sun and rain.

Today, though, activity on the floor is considerably more benign than it was in Roman times. Usually, there are a few elderly men playing boules, and groups of kids kicking soccer balls back and forth. I return there by myself from time to time and always take visitors to see it. During nice weather, it's a good place to relax quietly with a sandwich and a bottle of wine while sitting on the stone bleachers in the warm sunshine. And the jazz record store is still there—right across the street.

During the first two centuries of Roman rule, when their legions had beaten menacing German tribes back across the Rhine, Paris was a peaceful place. The growing villages on the islands in the Seine and along the left bank of the river didn't have walls until the third century, when Roman power had waned. But even during the Roman era, these small settlements along the Seine had qualities that we associate with Paris today. One is a deeply embedded classicism, present in art and in literature but most visible in Parisian architecture. The Parisii, the Gallic people for whom the city is named, believed that the goddess Athena had saved Paris, son of the king of Troy, when the Greeks sacked the city. She brought him and a few followers to the Seine. So, in the minds of the Parisii, they were the direct descendants of the first classical civilization. The Romans who faced the Parisii also thought their city had been founded by a member of Trojan royalty, Aeneas, who also escaped the doomed city and made his way to the Tiber. So, in the minds of the Romans, they, too, were descended from that first classical civilization. The Roman ruins that remain in Paris, especially the Arènes and the Thermes de Cluny, are classically inspired, as are most of the public buildings in Paris built before the twentieth century. The National Assembly is only one example. And, just as today's Paris does, Roman Paris contained many impressive shops, especially on the Île de la Cité. Boats of various descriptions brought grains, meats, and fish from the countryside down the river, as well as cheeses and fine wines. Paris had its luxurious and sensual appeal from the beginning.

.   .   .

I left the Arènes and continued my wandering. I began to climb an attractive double staircase on the rue Monge. A few steps up, I found a fountain from the seventeenth century that had once been connected to a Roman aqueduct that brought water to this then peripheral neighborhood of Paris. From there, the staircase rose about two stories to the rue Rollin. It was peaceful but dull, and hardly worth the climb, although I did find a marker on one building that said Descartes had lived there.

For the next quarter-hour, I walked along mostly empty streets. On a corner of the rue Lhomond, I was pondering which way to go next when an elderly gentleman stopped to ask me if I was visiting this "quartier." I said yes, and he told me I should visit the church just down the street, at number 30. When I peered down the empty street, I saw no sign of a church. "Oh yes, it's there," he said. "Just ring the bell and say hello to the old woman on your right, and go into the chapel." Then he added, in a jovial but odd way, "It's not a Roman Catholic church, but we are all Roman Catholics." With a jaunty wave he moved on.

I wondered what he could have meant, and was curious enough to walk down the forbidding, empty rue Lhomond to number 30, where I found two heavy wooden doors firmly closed. On the stone wall to the right was a small brass marker that read "Congrégation du Saint-Esprit." A heavy iron knocker hung on one door, but, sure enough, there was a button in the mounting of the knocker. When I pushed it, a bell rang and the door opened onto a featureless hallway. There was indeed an old woman, in an office behind a window on my right. She pointed me toward a door. Behind it, I found myself alone in a small domed, arched, rococo chapel with beautiful stained glass. Along the walls stood full-sized statues of saints. Every transom held a painting, and behind the altar, surrounded by sculpted clouds, was a statue of Mary holding the baby Jesus on her hip. Both she and her child were wearing onion-shaped gold crowns. The chapel wasn't kitsch, although a more jaded eye might think that it was. To me there was an absolute sincerity behind all the ornamentation that made it mysterious and moving. I found out later that the members of the Congrégation du Saint-Esprit were known as Spiritains. They are indeed Roman Catholic, but Catholics with an evangelical purpose among the poor in the undeveloped world, especially in Africa. There are about twenty-six hundred professed adherents worldwide, including about three hundred in France. But more people than that attend the services. Unfortunately, some of their missionaries have lately been accused of sexual abuse.

As I left, I opened a door that I thought led out but that in fact led into the office of the old woman. She recoiled immediately and pushed her chair away from me. "Oh non," she said. "Non, non, non." She was shaking and white with terror. Apologizing, I retreated and went out another door to the street. I was a little shaken myself. I had never ignited such fear in anyone. And why didn't she recognize me? I had entered just ten minutes or so before. Perhaps she had been lost in some reverie, and I was a sudden, startling apparition just inside her door.

After that, I walked back and forth across the rue Mouffe-

tard, where Tracy and I had wandered on our last night together
in Paris. I walked down narrow streets that have survived since
medieval times, climbing uphill past raucous cafés, crêperies,
bakeries, butcher shops, cheese vendors, and produce stands.
Sometimes, along the second stories, there were still signs in
the ancient plaster for taverns that disappeared centuries ago.
In one house, during a renovation in the 1930s, the workers
found a cache of several thousand gold coins from the era of
Louis XV.

At the foot of the rue Mouffetard, I turned onto the rue
Broca. It goes under the Boulevard de Port-Royal and on to the
Boulevard Arago, which is very wide and lined with tall chestnut trees. There I found the Cité Fleurie. The gate was locked,
but I peered through the bars. Now it's a nationally protected
monument, but in the late 1890s it was cheap housing where
Gauguin, Modigliani, Picasso, and other artists lived. Farther
down the boulevard, I saw the thick, hulking, featureless walls
of La Santé Prison, which had just closed for renovation. Occasionally, there were plaques on the walls honoring the Jewish
schoolchildren or the resistance fighters who were executed
there during the Occupation. In 1986, a woman named Nadine
Vaujour landed a helicopter on the roof of one of the buildings.
Her husband, Michel Vaujour, climbed aboard, and the two
flew off. He wasn't recaptured until several months later. The
only remaining pissoir (public urinal) in Paris stands on the
sidewalk beside the prison. It's all rusted and has fallen in on
itself. The two ugliest sites in Paris can be captured in a single
photograph.

The Boulevard Arago runs along a fenced park on the
southern side of the Paris Observatory. Feral cats, a lot of them,
all black and white, crouched under foliage and stared out at me

suspiciously; a few feline generations ago, there must have been a huge, dominant black-and-white male. Along the rue du Faubourg Saint-Jacques, which runs between two major hospitals, I saw small coveys of nuns out for a walk, many of them African, talking serenely among themselves, apart from the world. When at last I arrived back at my apartment, I had been gone more than five hours.

That night, a strange event occurred. As I lay in my bed, almost asleep, I heard Tracy's voice calling to me: "Greg. Greg." I opened my eyes and pushed myself up off my pillow. I saw her sitting at the end of the bed. She was wearing a filmy white gown. She didn't speak again. She sat slightly sideways to me, leaning back a little on her right arm, her head turned so she could look directly at me. I looked directly at her. Our eyes met, and I could see into them, just as if she were alive. It was really her. Her face glowed a little, but she was not moving at all. It was not frightening. I reached toward her, and she disappeared.

For several moments, I stared into the darkness where she had been. Then I lay back on the pillow and looked up at the ceiling. I felt completely at peace. She had come to Paris with me again.

CHAPTER ELEVEN

A Message from Céleste

During those months in Paris during the spring of 2014, while I was attending the language school at the Sorbonne, I felt that I was living in a world I had imagined. My apartment was real enough, as was the daily walk past Marshal Ney's statue to the school. So were my classes at school, and so was memorizing verb conjugations in the evening after dinner. But the question "Am I really doing this?" frequently came to me during the many hours I spent alone in the apartment or walking the streets of Paris at random.

Monday through Friday, I had a two-hour grammar class that began at noon. In the morning, I had breakfast, dressed, and studied until about eleven, when I ate lunch. That was often pâté thickly spread on pieces of baguette and apple slices. I left about eleven-thirty to walk to school. I had been placed in a class of mid-level students. Despite my sincere and dedicated effort, I was far from the best student in the class. Building a usable vocabulary took some work, but that work was just brute memorization. Learning grammar required memorization, too, but it also required judgment. Proper French consists of thousands upon thousands of small details. There are grammatical and orthographic rules that lurk silently, ready to bite if you misuse them or, worse, forget them entirely. I was bitten more than most of my classmates.

After the grammar class, I had a one-hour phonics class, beginning at two-thirty. That class was humbling. For complicated reasons, I was put in a section where the other students' French was noticeably better than mine. The teacher was a tall, slender, theatrical woman who had the most lovely speaking voice. Hearing her recite a sentence was an aesthetic experience, even though at first I had no idea what she was saying. I sat in terror that she would call on me— *"Grégoire!"*—to recite a phonetic exercise such as saying "sur, sœur, sourd" (on, sister, deaf) with the vowels pronounced correctly. But the torture and the fear were valuable. After six or eight weeks, I could tell that I heard and understood more than before, although still not everything. Near the end of the semester, the teacher began a class by asking me how I pronounced my "r"s. "Avec espoir, madame," I said (with hope). It caught her off guard. After a moment's pause, she laughed and the class laughed, too. But my response was true enough.

I am sure that I was the oldest student at the school— I would turn seventy that December—which made me either an object of curiosity for the other students or, just as often, a puzzling phenomenon who could be easily ignored. For my part, I was reserved most of the time, especially around the young women. Most of them were fresh and pretty but also forty-five or fifty years younger than I was. Knowing that none of them would want me for a boyfriend or even for a date, I never said or did anything that was forward or remotely suggestive. After a week or so in class, the other students saw that I wasn't up to anything but learning French. They relaxed around me, and I was able to make friends.

Yulia, a stately Russian beauty, sat in front of me. Her husband worked at the Parc des Expositions and got free tickets to the shows there. She surprised me one day in February with a ticket to Le Salon de l'Agriculture, which I'll talk about directly. Claire, from Tyler, Texas, sat behind me, and Anja, from Copenhagen, sat beside Claire. We three became good pals. I took them for kir vin blanc at La Coupole. I showed them the photographs of Hemingway beside the bar and talked to them a little about Paris in the twenties, about which they knew nothing.

Late in May, I took them to Au Moulin à Vent, on the rue des Fossés Saint-Bernard, as a farewell dinner. Claire and I ganged up on Anja to make her try escargot, a signature dish there. The matronly waitress put the plate down in front of Anja. She looked in horror at the snails swimming in butter and garlic, and her face flushed intensely red.

"Elle est débutante?" the waitress asked. We said that, yes, this was her first time, and the waitress stood by to watch. Anja's protests attracted the attention of people at the tables nearby, who called out to encourage her. Anja was so red by now that you could almost feel the heat coming off her cheeks and forehead.

"Take a bite of bread," I said. "Then eat the snail, and then take another bite of bread."

Claire pierced one of the snails with a fork. Anja took a bite of bread, but as she did so, Claire stuck the snail in her mouth. Anja was startled; her eyes grew huge. She swallowed hard, almost involuntarily, and the snail went down. As the restaurant responded with polite applause, Claire and I finished the escargots.

One day, after my grammar class, as I was gathering my papers and putting on my coat, I was the last student still in the room. The kindly instructor, whose husband I later learned was a relatively well-known author of comic verse, asked me if my wife was with me in Paris. I said, "Non. Je suis veuf." (No, I'm a widower.) Her smile immediately disappeared in embarrassment. She apologized and expressed condolences. I assured her that I had not taken offense. But that was one of the very few personal moments that occurred the whole semester.

Many days, I came home after my classes were over, dropped off my books, and set out on random walks around Paris. Sometimes I walked for an hour or two, sometimes for six or seven hours. I was never tired, and never bored, which actually increased my sense of being someone else inside a transparent bubble. Paris was not at all hostile, but Paris didn't care whether I was there or not. Strangely, Paris almost seemed to disappear unless I went out into the streets looking for what I might find.

One afternoon, I happened upon the entrance to the Jardin des Plantes. Since it was still early in the year, nothing was in bloom. Only two or three other people were there. I wandered around its long expanse, thinking how pretty it must be when spring brought out the flowers. And that turned out to be true. It was pretty when I returned eight weeks later, but it was also so crowded that walking aimlessly in a reverie was impossible, and I felt myself perversely longing for the gray February afternoon when I had been there practically alone. That afternoon, I had also entered the zoo that runs along the northern border of the Jardin. The last time I had been in a zoo was years earlier, in San Antonio, with Tracy, Vivian, and Ben. We had all ridden on an elephant. There were no elephants here, but there was a snow leopard, a snowy owl, a yak, an oryx, and a warthog. There were red pandas, who were adorable-looking but scuffled with each other constantly, and an impressive variety of colorful, exotic birds. But the animals that thrilled me most were the small herd of Przewalski's horses. These are the closest existing relatives of the breed of horses that lived at the time of the prehistoric cave painters. Almost extinct at one time, they were preserved in captivity and have been successfully reintroduced into their native Mongolia. Though they're thick and compact, like burros, they have a horse's dignity. They look like a cave painting come to life.

One afternoon in early March, I used the ticket Yulia had given me to go to Le Salon de l'Agriculture. I don't think I would have gone except for the free ticket, but now I never miss it when I'm in Paris. It is, in effect, the state fair of France. The salon was spread out across nine immense halls. Forced to choose among them, I did not go into the pavilion dedicated to fruits, vegetables, grains, plants, and flowers, or the pavilion that displayed agricultural machinery and methods. I felt a little sorry to ignore the pavilion dedicated to birds, fowl, and poultry, and immensely sorry when I turned away from the pavilion dedicated entirely to dogs and cats and the one with foods from other countries. I wondered what might be there from the United States—Texas barbecue? Fritos?

Instead, I entered the pavilion dedicated to horses and other livestock. I did not know there were so many different breeds of horses, from huge, thick draft horses like the Percherons, which weighed over a ton and had long, hanging fur around their hooves, to the tiniest, most delicate miniature horses imaginable, three or four of whom fit easily in a normal-sized stall. There were cattle, too—immense, lumbering bulls whose testicles looked like two eggplants in a net—and tiny goats, the size of cocker spaniels, whose elaborate horns curved around themselves in circles. Some of the hogs were the size of rhinos. Most of them were lying on their side, exhausted from supporting their great mass on tiny legs. Once, a farm boy picked up a suckling piglet by a hind leg; it squealed in anguished terror at being jerked away from its mama.

And, of course, I went to the pavilion for the foods of France. It was so vast that I was lost from the moment I entered until three hours later, when it took me another half-hour to find my way out. I wandered around, sampling cheeses, hams, wines, liquors, juices, syrups, jellies, beers, breads, candies, cakes, and even French bourbon. Best of all was a small glass of Armagnac that had just recently been bottled but had been aging in a cask since 1978. It tasted as if it had been lying dormant all that time, waiting for this moment to burst into flavor in my mouth. A bottle cost sixty euros. I was tempted but didn't succumb.

The zoo and the salon were glorious exceptions to the calmer, random pleasures of most of my walks. As I walked along across block after block, it was small, ephemeral moments that counted most of all—a border collie waiting expectantly outside a pâtisserie, the window of a shop filled with nothing but antique barometers, a round woman in a shawl begging on a street corner while talking on her cell phone, a mother calling down the street to her dawdling child, the elderly woman in a wool coat asking me with extreme politeness where she might find the rue Broca (and I knew!), the plaque above the door to an apartment saying that Verlaine had lived there, a covered arcade of exclusive shops, the narrow cobbled street where I came across a fenced pen containing goats and chickens. I rarely found a street with nothing of interest, and when I did, *that* became interesting. What is it, I wondered, that makes it lack interest?

Why was I doing this? I didn't know exactly. The easy, obvious answer would be that I was searching for something or someone, that Tracy's death had severed my moorings and now I was condemned to wandering until I found a safe harbor. But that didn't seem right to me at the time, and still doesn't seem right as I consider it now. It's true that I was compelled to go out and observe Paris, but that is not the same thing as searching Paris for something particular. I did not feel that I was searching at all. When I came home, I rarely had anything more with me than what I had had when I left, except for books, which I could not resist buying. Certainly, I would have been disappointed if I had searched for hours and not found what I was looking for, but I felt no disappointment. In fact, I didn't mind at all. Yes, I was alone in Paris, but during my walks I was alone *with* Paris, which was where I wanted to be and had chosen to be. Paris asked for nothing from me, and all I asked of Paris was just to be Paris. That, I believed, was our understanding.

In addition to my solitary walks, I was drawn toward the grand museums in Paris and the paintings on their walls. I found that I could lose myself while walking in museums much as I lost myself walking along the sidewalks in Paris. Tracy had known more about art than I did. She knew the basic history—her thick and tattered copy of Janson's *History of Art* from her student days was on our bookshelves at home—and she also had an acute, instinctive understanding of composition and color. As we walked through a museum, she did the talking. I hardly knew enough to ask questions. She liked Cézanne in particular, understanding the complicated geometry in his landscapes and loving the play of light in his often muted palette of browns and greens. One of the reasons she had wanted to visit Aix was to see his studio there. It was much larger and taller than she had imagined, and naturally lit by a wall of glass windows. On a mantel were three skulls that he used in a late painting; a large collection of pottery sat on a high shelf; a rickety wooden stepladder went twenty feet or more up to the ceiling. Evidently, Cézanne trusted it, but I wasn't sure I would have. A large crucifix hung on the wall above the shelf of pottery, evidence of his deeply felt Catholicism. The studio itself seemed to be a shrine devoted to serious work and deep contemplation. "With an apple," Cézanne once remarked, "I will astonish Paris."

Now in Paris myself, but without Tracy to guide me, I decided that perhaps I could strengthen the bond between the city and myself by joining both the Louvre and the Musée d'Orsay. My membership cards gave me free admission and allowed me to skip the frequently long lines waiting to enter. Before joining, I had visited the museums only occasionally and stayed as long as I could. But now I made more frequent, shorter visits. I found that spending about two hours was ideal. When I stayed longer than that, the art melded into a blur and my response to any single work was dulled. Sometimes I knew which work I would go see first, but often I would leave that to chance. Either way, I seldom had a goal during a visit to a museum, just as I seldom had a goal during my long walks. In my wanderings about a museum, something would occur, most often a strong reaction to a new discovery, that let me know that this visit was over. Although I hadn't known in advance what it would be, I had now seen what I had come to see and found what I had come to find. I always left with a great feeling of plenitude and fulfillment.

The first painting that affected me deeply and seemed to speak personally to me was not one of the many famous masterpieces in those museums, but *Le Veuf* by Jean-Louis Forain, from 1885, which is in the Musée d'Orsay. Forain had lived in bohemian poverty in Paris as a young man, and had even shared a room for several months with Arthur Rimbaud. Later, he had a long friendship with Degas. He made his living from his painting but also from his very popular political cartoons and drawings of scenes of contemporary life, which were published in a variety of newspapers. In *Le Veuf,* a tall, slender bourgeois gentleman in a black top hat and a black suit—we presume that he has just returned from his wife's funeral—is seated in a stuffed chair with narrow orange stripes in what must have been her boudoir. His left elbow is on his knee, and his chin is in his left hand, as he stares pensively at the shelves of a cabinet that hold white, lacy women's undergarments. One such garment dangles from his right hand to the floor. These were his wife's most intimate possessions, but what should he do with them? To throw them away would be an affront to her memory. But to give them away, so that another woman could wear them, would be an affront as well. All this lace is filled with associations for him, but without her, those associations would lead only to emptiness. Although the painting is full of objects—boxes and cabinets and lace and stuffed chairs—emptiness is the main impression it gives. Forain married Jeanne Bosc, also a painter, in 1891, when he was thirty-nine. They had a long, happy marriage that ended only with his

death, in 1931. *Le Veuf,* then, painted six years before his marriage, does not come from Forain's personal experience. But he
was able to imagine the personal experience of another man, a
man like me, for example, with accuracy and compassion. I lin-
ger in front of the painting whenever I visit the Musée d'Orsay.

By now, I had read enough and seen enough so that I wasn't
completely naïve about art. I had written a book about the *Venus
de Milo,* and one about the paintings in prehistoric caves. But
my knowledge was specific and limited, and I knew that Tracy
had seen art differently and better than I did. Whereas she saw
paintings as forms and colors, my response to paintings was to
see them as narratives. That reaction is reasonable for paintings
like *Le Veuf* and for a huge variety of religious scenes, domestic
scenes, battle scenes, and so on. But that is not a reaction that
makes much sense when looking at an abstract painting or one
of Cézanne's landscapes, or even a portrait like the *Mona Lisa*.
I wanted to learn how to look at a painting *without* imagining a
narrative. And early that spring in Paris, I had a piece of luck.
I found a series of lectures on nineteenth- and early-twentieth-
century French paintings listed in one of the museum bulletins.
The lectures were once a week, in the late afternoon, so there
was no conflict with any of my classes. Although the lectures
were in French, I found I could follow them without too much
difficulty. I was soon enraptured by what I was seeing and
learning.

The lecturer was a slender woman in her early fifties who
had a mass of wavy reddish-brown hair that looked cared for
but also untamed. I liked it. She had the appearance of having dressed and done her hair while she was slightly distracted.
Every Tuesday afternoon, she sat at a table on a stage in the
front of the lecture hall and plugged a flash drive into a com-

puter connected to two large screens, one on either side of
the stage. She began speaking exactly at four-thirty without
any introduction or call to order, and the room immediately
became quiet. She continued without pause until six. She had
a clear, soft, musical voice, and radiated a calm authority and
a complete certainty about her remarks. About two hundred
people attended these lectures, most of them in their twenties
and probably students. There had been an easy registration
procedure, little more than a formality, but the students could
get college credit for attending. When she finished a lecture,
everyone politely applauded. In these pages, she will be called
Céleste Bernard.

I always sat in the same seat, in the second row, on the right
side of the hall. Her course began with David, Ingres, and Neo-
classicism and then proceeded to Romanticism, and then the
Barbizon school, which I knew a little bit about from staying in
Barbizon with Tracy while stag hunting, and continued chron-
ologically with Impressionism, Postimpressionism, Gauguin
and the Pont-Aven school, the Nabis, Fauvism, Cubism,
and finally the Surrealists. She was particularly good on van
Gogh. She had a magnified photograph of some details in one
of his canvasses, which she used to explain what she called his
"touch"—that is, the exact way he made his brushstrokes. And
she added that his ecstatic paintings of nature are very much in
a Dutch tradition. In the Netherlands, there were many fewer
Biblical images in painting because in the Calvinist religion the
representation of God was accomplished by a celebration of His
creation, of nature and the world that surrounds us. And she
cast van Gogh—rapid, spontaneous, emotional, reactive, concerned with color—as the opposite of Cézanne—slow, intellectual, pensive, concerned with shapes. She also compared van

Gogh with Seurat. In some ways, especially in their colors, it's easy to see the links between them. On the other hand, if there was ever a painter completely opposed to spontaneity, it was Seurat. And she showed us the importance of lines in Seurat, which is not the first thing one would say about van Gogh.

She was rapturous about Puvis de Chavannes, who is often overlooked because he is unique and can't be easily grouped with any school. His paintings are filled with idealized but enigmatic personages who seem almost like marble statues and, she said, push the spectator toward meditation and reverie. She spoke of the "fury" in Delacroix's work, and the high literary quality of his journals. She showed us Sérusier's *The Talisman*. He had come to Pont-Aven and, challenged and prodded by Gauguin, had painted *The Talisman,* the first painting whose subject was color itself. And then she spoke of Monet as the supreme colorist.

It was a magnificent course. She was so quiet and unassuming, but also completely confident. Each lecture was filled with knowledge and perception. She could look at a painting and tell you exactly what she saw and what was there for you to see. That may sound simple, but not everyone can do it, not even every art critic. It was an ability I had always admired in Tracy.

We had to turn in a paper during the last class. I wrote mine on van Gogh's final days, still a subject that interests me. During that last class, there was also a test. Most of the questions asked us to identify a painting and name the painter. It wasn't too difficult. When we finished, we handed her our tests and our papers and left. As I handed her mine, I thanked her for an excellent course. She simply nodded, smiled, and said, "Merci," almost in a whisper. That was the only time I spoke to her that semester. I left feeling quite sad that the course was over.

When I returned to Austin in June, I decided to send
Céleste Bernard copies of my books. I searched the Web, trying to find an e-mail address or a physical address for her, but
found nothing and gave up with a shrug. Then, two weeks
later, on July 18, I was stunned to find a message from her in
my inbox. She could have found my e-mail address among the
registration forms, or it might have been that we had to include
our e-mails on our paper and test. At any rate, there the message was on my computer screen, written in French. It began
with a simple "Bonjour" and no other salutation. She said she
was contacting me to congratulate me on my results on the test.
She suggested a book about van Gogh—*Van Gogh: Le Soleil
en face,* by Pascal Bonafoux. She said she would be in Paris all
summer giving lectures—"The Painters of Montparnasse,"
"The Avant-Garde at the Beginning of the Twentieth Century," and "Paris in the Fifties." Despite these lectures, she had
extra time during the summer and liked to meet with former
students who were still in France, to hear their critiques and
commentaries, so she could improve her courses. She also said
she was an Anglophile—Oscar Wilde was her favorite British
writer—and would like to discuss literature with me in English
or in French. She signed her message "Céleste Bernard."

My first reaction was despair over not having stayed in
Paris after the course, even though I knew that would have
been impossible. I had had to vacate my apartment, for one
thing, and then there was a long list of rational reasons for
returning home. But I wrote her back that very day, address-
ing her as "Chère Mme Bernard." I told her that I wasn't in
Paris any longer; I had had to return home because I had work
to do at the University of Texas. I told her that I had been free
to come to Paris because my wife had died more than three

years ago and my children were grown and on their own. After some deliberation, I admitted that I had tried unsuccessfully to find her e-mail address, taking a chance that this would be welcome news rather than making her uncomfortable. I said that I had searched for her address because I wanted to send her my books, and that I would still like to send them to her. I added that I would very much like to begin an exchange with her on English and French literature, and that my three favorite French writers were Balzac, Georges Simenon, and La Rochefoucauld, which seemed like a bizarre trio to me then, and now still seems bizarre, although defensible. I signed the message "Greg."

I didn't hear from her until four days later, on the 22nd, when I was relieved to receive a long message. Once again it began simply "Bonjour." It contained some information but was not especially personal. She had traveled in the United States from Niagara Falls to Yosemite and from New York to Los Angeles, and her main impressions seemed to have been of size and space, of largeness compared with smallness in France. She found the whole country both appealing and disorienting. As for my strange trio of authors, she said she liked Balzac for his characters and his descriptions of Paris, but she preferred Maupassant and Flaubert. She hadn't read La Rochefoucauld, and added, "I know that Simenon is well appreciated by Anglo-Saxons," a statement I found curious but charming. I rarely thought of myself and my family and friends as Anglo-Saxons, but I suppose we are. She asked me directly about my writing and my work at the university. She concluded by telling me that I wouldn't lose the French I'd learned if I would practice a little each day. That made me smile. "Yes, teacher," I thought. Once again, she signed the message simply "Céleste Bernard."

I answered several days later with a rather long message addressed to "Chère madame." Writing in French took a long time, as I searched a dictionary for the proper word and a grammar for correct usage. I'm certain I made plenty of mistakes despite my best efforts. But, I told myself, I was practicing a little each day. French has a formal pronoun "vous," which means "you," and is used in most situations. There is also an informal pronoun "tu," which also means "you" and is used among family and friends. At the end of my message, I said that I wasn't sure in France how one goes from formality to less formality, but that I wished she would call me "Greg" and use "tu" with me as well.

When her next message arrived, I was very pleased that it began "Cher Greg."

This time, she included her mailing address so I could send her my books, and the whole message was more relaxed and personal than the first two. She lived near the Parc Monceau, which I should have gone to see during my stay but never did. She loved it. She walked there often on her way to go swimming. "I dream a little while crossing it," she said. "I adore nature, trees, and flowers." She was soon going to the south of France to visit her mother, sister, and brother, but she preferred Normandy and Brittany, in the north, with their steep cliffs and solitary beaches and changing skies. She included four photographs to show me what she meant. "It's astonishing," she said, "that we can talk like this even though an ocean and so many kilometers separate us." She used "tu" in its various forms throughout her message—never the formal "vous"— and signed it "Céleste."

After this we began to exchange longer messages that usually contained photographs and details about our lives. She had been separated from her husband for five years. She had a large apartment in Paris, where she lived with her daughter, who was twenty-one and worked in graphic design. She and her daughter were "cohabitants," as she put it, and lived independent lives. When the girl was younger, they had frequently traded apartments with couples who lived in other countries in Europe or in the United States, where they had spent many months. Her daughter had learned English by watching American children's shows on television.

Céleste was born in the countryside south of Paris. She'd loved painting and nature from the time she was young, and had had a blissful childhood. Her father and grandfather maintained a large garden of flowers and vegetables, where she spent many hours studying the plants as they grew and transformed according to the season. She loved the way the light changed with every season and at different times of the day. Even insects and small animals fascinated her.

Then, in adolescence, her life became difficult. She lost faith in religion. Her father, who was stern and deeply religious, judged her lack of faith severely. Rebellious, she left home at eighteen and became a nurse, and then worked for Johnson & Johnson, selling surgical supplies. Although her work required her to travel throughout France, which she enjoyed, she was miserable otherwise. In the evening, she took courses in drawing and read books and spent time in dreamy reveries, in an effort to forget her tiresome and unrewarding daily life.

She was almost thirty when she met her husband. They quickly had a child. Since her job often required her to travel for whole weeks at a time, she quit working to take care of her daughter. Now living in Paris, and wanting never to return to working in medicine, she decided to go to school. She thought

of studying painting but worried that she would never find
work, so she studied the history of art instead, at the Louvre
and the Sorbonne. These studies weren't always easy, since she
had to choose courses according to the hours when they were
offered and not according to subjects that really interested her.
But she persisted, and obtained a master's degree, all the while
raising her daughter. At last, she had the qualifications to start
her life as a teacher and lecturer on art, and she had time to
paint besides. She had abandoned one life she hated and created
a new one that made her happy. And she had reconciled with
her family long ago. Her father had since passed away, and her
mother now lived in the south, near Céleste's brother.

We talked a lot about books. She had in fact read very
widely. I sent her a copy of my book on the *Venus de Milo,* and
because I mentioned Larry McMurtry she ordered a copy of
Duane est dépressif. "It's astonishing, impossible to imagine less
than a month ago," she wrote, "that I would correspond with
you, that I would read Larry McMurtry (whom I had never
heard of), and that I would read your book on the *Venus de
Milo.* Life is very strange and holds nice surprises!" Then she
surprised me with an invitation: "If you are able to take some
days of vacation this summer, why wouldn't you come refresh
yourself in Europe?" She was going to paint at a studio in the
country. "There is a small house decorated as of old with furniture from the Normandy of yesterday. There are three bedrooms and plenty of space. You would be able to read and write
while I would paint in the studio. And we would explore the
region together."

I had been puzzling over how we could see each other
again. Inviting her to Austin was my first thought, but it didn't
seem to me that we had reached a point where we would both

be comfortable in Austin together, whether she stayed with me or in a hotel. I speculated that perhaps by fall a visit to Austin would be comfortable for us both. And by then the weather would be cooler, I could show her the countryside, and we could drive to see the museums in Houston and Fort Worth. Still, I couldn't quite see it. But now that didn't matter. She had filled the vacuum of the huge distance between us by sending me this invitation.

It was the second week in July. I wrote her that I would be very pleased to come back to Paris, but I couldn't leave for a week or so, and then school would start during the last week of August. She wrote back suggesting five days in early August that would be convenient for her. Could I come then? Yes, I could. I bought my tickets. Was there a hotel near her apartment where I could stay? No, that wasn't necessary. I could stay in her apartment, in her daughter's room. Also, there was no need to take a cab from the airport. She would drive to Charles de Gaulle and meet me at the gate.

CHAPTER TWELVE

Le Horla

Although I had flown across an ocean all the way to Paris to see her, when I was at last on the ground at Charles de Gaulle and waiting in line at the passport control, I began to doubt that any of this was real. I prepared myself to find nobody at all waiting for me inside the airport. But once I was through the passport control, and after a bored customs officer waved me past his desk without bothering even to glance at my suitcase, I emerged into the multinational crowds and the incessant multilingual babble of a concourse at Charles de Gaulle. Céleste was there, in the midst of it all, shyly smiling. She was wearing a white blouse and a trim skirt printed with red roses. Our greeting was a little awkward, but not too awkward. We acted as if we were friends or business associates, and she was picking me up as a favor. We shook hands.

She asked about the flight as we walked to her car. It was about ten-thirty on a warm, sunny August morning. I had slept only a little, if at all, during the flight, but I didn't feel tired. I was very concentrated on her, without knowing what to say. She spoke hardly any English, as it turned out, and I was self-conscious about my French, even after a semester at the school. I knew that most of what I said in French was halting and faulty. Nevertheless, we did manage some chitchat and some easy laughs. She acted as if all this was a normal part of a well-established routine, by which she often came to Charles de Gaulle to pick me up. For me, every impression was new. I had never been in a parking lot at Charles de Gaulle. I didn't know for certain that there *were* parking lots there. But now I was standing by a parking space among hundreds of vehicles as I waited on the passenger side of her blue Toyota while she unlocked the driver's side door. Everything was mundane and dreamlike all at once.

As she drove into Paris, I was able to look at her closely for the first time. Her eyes were the same red-brown color as her thick and still-untamed hair. She had fair skin and wore little or no makeup. Except for her eyes, the most distinguishing feature of her face was her long, straight mouth. Altogether, she was slender and pretty and feminine. Her skirt stopped above her knees. I liked seeing her bare legs move as her right foot reached for the gas pedal or the brake.

Her apartment was on a quiet, unremarkable street in the Eighth Arrondissement, in north-central Paris, not far from her beloved Parc Monceau. She found a parking spot close to the door of her building. She and I and my suitcase crowded together in the tiny elevator as our bodies were pressed ever so slightly together.

She unlocked the door of her apartment and asked me to take off my shoes, as she did the same. Just inside the door was a heavy wooden armoire that looked as if it had been in her family for generations. To the right was her bedroom; to the left, the kitchen and a hallway that led to the bathroom and her daughter's bedroom, where I was to sleep. Straight ahead was a bright living room with a sofa and stuffed chairs and an alcove where she worked on her watercolors. There was a large folding screen painted with roses beside a fireplace with a marble mantel. A huge framed mirror was mounted on the wall above it. Vases filled with flowers were everywhere. White lace curtains hung by the windows, which opened onto the street. Flower boxes filled with green plants were attached to the black iron railing of the balcony.

She had told me on the way from the airport that she would have to pick up her sister at the Gare de Lyon. I assumed we would do that together, later in the afternoon. But after only five minutes or so, she said she needed to leave or she would be late. She put on her shoes again—they were multicolored designer sneakers—and disappeared out the door. Silence descended. I didn't move. After just over an hour back in Paris, I was alone in her apartment. Now what?

Almost immediately I discovered that I wasn't entirely alone. A brown-and-gray-spotted cat, who was hiding under the sofa in the living room, peered at me intently, waiting to see what I would do next. I decided to look around, starting with her bedroom. She slept on a low, narrow cot that was pushed against a wall. It looked like something one might find in a cell in a convent. There was a large closet with sliding doors against one wall. I went back to the living room and then looked at the watercolors in progress in her studio. They were either landscapes or detailed botanical studies of leaves, grasses, and flowers. They were exquisite, very assured and masterful. I understood now that her lectures were strengthened by her own skill as a painter. She had confronted problems in color and composition in her own work and could understand how other painters had solved similar problems.

I was glad to see that her daughter's room had a larger, more comfortable bed than Céleste's cot. Her daughter was off at an internship in Germany. The bathroom was quite large. Isolated in the center stood an immaculate, gleaming white enamel bathtub on legs. Thick white towels were folded on a stool at the side of the tub. Boxes, bottles, tubes of lotions, salts, powders, and oils waited on a second stool, near the first. On the opposite side of the tub was a folding wooden rack where several items of pretty and delicate lingerie had been hung to dry. This hidden enclave of sensuality fueled my imagination. I imagined seeing a nude Céleste sinking into the tub, where scented oils floated in steamy water.

Back in the living room, I tried and failed to get the cat to come to me. I would have liked to explore the neighborhood, but I couldn't leave, because I had no way to get back into the apartment. With nothing better to do, I read a book I had brought with me on the airplane.

Later in the afternoon, Céleste returned alone: her sister was staying with a friend, and she had dropped her off there. There was a café Céleste liked on the other side of the Parc Monceau where we could have dinner. Outside, it had become overcast and looked like rain, but the somber sky did nothing to diminish the appeal of the park as we entered. In fact, the threat of bad weather made it even more romantic, since almost no one was there except for the two of us. It became our own special province.

The Parc Monceau is surrounded by some of the most elegant private mansions in Paris. The area was open meadows when the village of Monceau was annexed during the Second Empire. Immediately afterward, just as American developers of pricy suburbs place their houses around a golf course, the land

around the park was sold as locations for large family houses to
the very rich, with the added incentive that the owners of the
surrounding houses would have a key to enter the park at night,
after it was closed to the public. In the spring, when flowers are
blooming, it is probably the most beautiful public area in Paris.
It is dotted with serene ponds and charming stone bridges that
go from nowhere to nowhere. All around there are faux ruins,
broken Greek columns from an imaginary temple to Mars, a
much-scaled-down Egyptian pyramid, and a huge stone arch
that was once the entrance to the City Hall of Paris. There are
swings and slides and sandboxes for children, grassy meadows where people lounge on blankets during nice weather, and
monuments tucked here and there to grand figures like Chopin
and Maupassant, whose monument is a little odd. His head is
on top of a pedestal, looking down on a reclining woman in a
clinging robe who is lost in reverie. The book she was reading,
presumably one of Maupassant's, dangles in her left hand. Has
it put her to sleep?

Maupassant's monument had recently been cleaned and
was snowy white. As Céleste and I looked at the swooning
woman, I began to think. I had come all this way at her invitation. Wasn't she hoping, even expecting, that various things
would happen? I certainly was. Shouldn't I be the one to initiate
something? And when would there be a better time? I leaned
down and kissed her. She did not turn away, as she would at a
much later time, but she didn't participate in the kiss, either. Her
mouth stayed straight, still, and closed. After a few moments, I
backed off and stood straight. We both acted as if nothing had
happened and walked on through the lovely park to the café.

I could not find that café again today, even knowing that
it is somewhere on the west side of the park. Nor could I have

found it again at the time. I was simply following her. A light, misty rain began as we entered the café. Although there were only two or three occupied tables, it was warmly lit and felt comfortable. We sat at a table against a wall. When the waiter came, Céleste ordered easily, and I ordered not so easily, but, still, I did it. I was feeling two unexpected emotions—pride and relief. Pride because I was here in Paris, dining with an appealing Parisienne whom I had just kissed in a park without getting reproached or slapped. And relief because maybe all that meant I belonged here, or could belong here.

The light rain was still falling when we left the café. Céleste had found a newspaper lying on a seat next to us. She unfolded it and held it over her head like a scarf as she ran along the sidewalk, with me following behind. She couldn't run very fast because of her tight skirt, so her legs kicked out behind her at an angle. I didn't want to catch up with her, and lagged behind to watch her legs as she ran. Later, she wrote me that she felt young and giddy and romantic during this run home through the rain. And, in fact, she was flushed and a little out of breath when we reached the door of her building. Inside her apartment, she brought us both one of the white towels from the stool by the bathtub. We dried off a little, but neither of us was really very wet. We had a glass of wine, and talked for a while in the living room. Though it was not yet late, I began to feel the effects of my sleepless night on the airplane. I told her I was tired and needed to go to sleep. I rose from my chair, walked two steps to her chair, and bent to kiss her. Once again, she didn't turn away, but she didn't respond, either. Her lips stayed straight and tight. The next morning, we left Paris for the countryside.

She belonged to a society of watercolorists who studied

with a master who had a studio in the château she shared with
her husband. It was two hours or so west of Paris, in the Perche.
The château also contained rooms the students could rent while
they worked in the studio. Céleste had one of these, and she had
arranged for me to have a room as well for the three nights we
would be there.

She followed busy expressways to get out of Paris, but soon
we were on smaller highways that meandered through the rolling countryside. Beyond Paris, as I knew from my randonnées
on horseback, France is basically one huge farm. We drove
among perfectly tended fields of wheat and yellow canola, and
also skirted along the edges of forests. The Perche is famous
for horses. We passed impressive herds of huge Percheron draft
horses, like those I had seen at Le Salon de l'Agriculture. They
had thick, powerful legs and broad backs. As we passed by,
they continued idly grazing.

The château had two connected wings around a central
courtyard. One wing was devoted to the art studio, and the
other had accommodations for the artists. On one side was a
very large flower-and-vegetable garden. Three other artists
were there when we arrived, all of them women, and all with
their husbands. I was the only boyfriend, if that's what I was.
They were friendly with me, but reserved, and soon turned to
their own concerns. The women went to paint, two of the husbands went to work in the garden, and the third simply vanished. They all appeared completely indifferent to where I might
sleep—whether alone in my own room, or with Céleste in hers.

I spent the afternoon walking in the countryside, careful
not to get lost, which would have been easy to do. That evening,
we drove to a restaurant in a small town nearby for dinner. Her
afternoon of painting in the studio had put Céleste in an expan-

sive mood. She was really pleased with a still life of leaves and flowers she was working on. I could understand most of what she said. When I couldn't understand, I sometimes asked her to explain, but more often I just let it go. I could always understand enough to ask a question or make a comment that kept the conversation going.

The restaurant was in the center of the village. There was a small bookstore she liked just around the corner; we spent fifteen or twenty minutes there, looking at the books and talking about the ones we had read or wanted to read. As we were leaving, she picked up a copy of *Pierre et Jean* by Guy de Maupassant and said, "I want to buy this for you." I started to protest, but she shook her head, smiling, and said, "I want to. Let me do it." It was dark by the time we arrived back at the château. We said good night and quietly went to our separate rooms.

I have that book beside me on the desk as I write. I suppose I will keep it forever. And I still have the bookmark the clerk slipped between the pages as she handed the book to Céleste. I've often pondered what it might mean that she wanted me to have this particular novel. It's brilliant, and I read it with great pleasure. Céleste did—and does—love books. Perhaps there was nothing more to it than one reader's impulsive gift to another. In the novel, an adultery decades earlier destroys the relations between two brothers. And, further straining their relations, both brothers are attracted to their neighbor, Madame Rosémilly, who is a pretty young widow. Céleste wasn't a widow, but she was divorced. Or was she? I realized that I didn't know. Maybe, under French law, there were reasons to live separate lives without the complications of a divorce. I somewhat resembled Jean, the younger of the two brothers, who had light skin and hair, and eventually wins Madame Rosémilly. I saw

Céleste's husband in a photograph. He was dark, like Pierre, the older brother. The novel is convincing and enthralling on its own, but thoughts like these, even though I knew they were probably unwarranted, gave it a vivid, pointed reality for me.

. . .

The next afternoon, as I was reading *Pierre et Jean* in the courtyard, a hand covered each of my eyes and I heard Céleste say, "Guess who."

"Madame Pompadour."

"Ha! No, but you're close." And she laughed and kissed me on the cheek. That surprised me, since there were others in the courtyard to witness this small display of affection. That night, there was a communal dinner at the château that everyone had had a part in buying and preparing. My share was a couple bottles of wine and a monumental amount of peeling and slicing. There was still daylight when we finished eating, and Céleste wanted to take a walk. She drove us to a town where there was a well-known monastery with lovely gardens. We walked among them, talking quietly, while night fell.

The town and monastery were on a hillside. We climbed up a wide, paved sidewalk that curved around the hill, offering views across a broad valley. Lights from farmhouses flickered in the distance below us. When we passed a bench, Céleste said, "We could sit here for a while." We sat, and I embraced her, and this time she kissed me passionately. What had happened? What had I done since the day before to make her change her mind, to decide to open her lips instead of keeping them tight and straight? Or was this something she had imagined from the start? Had she always intended to mark time after my arrival until this night?

These questions came to me only during the long flight home a few days later, when I pondered all that had happened. At the time, I was overcome and so happy that I couldn't think at all. Her lips and her body pressed against mine consumed all my feelings. Why had I come back to Paris if not for this?

Back at the château, we climbed the curving wooden steps to her room as quietly as we could. A short time later, during some intense moments, she whispered a torrent of words into my ear. Her voice in a whisper was just as pleasing as when she spoke normally, but it was doubly intoxicating now, because I had no idea what she was saying. Later, we agreed that the bed was a little small for both of us to sleep together. I kissed her one last time and crept back down the stairs with my shoes in my hands.

The next day we acted like a couple as naturally as we could manage. She painted during the morning and afternoon, but we sat together during breakfast, lunch, and dinner. That evening, everyone at the château attended a concert of music by Berlioz in a church nearby. It was cold in that ancient sanctuary. I draped my jacket around her shoulders, and we listened with our hands entwined.

The next day, we returned to Paris. Her sister Marguerite had arrived at Céleste's apartment, where she was going to sleep on the couch. I liked her. She was a bright and lively scholar of medieval French texts. Though she hardly resembled Céleste at all, the two were obviously very close. Marguerite accepted me without hesitation. She asked me some questions about Texas and seemed to think it was the most natural thing in the world that I was there, staying with her sister in her apartment. Céleste cooked, and the three of us ate dinner around a tiny table in the kitchen. Afterward, when the dishes had been cleared, I did some card tricks for them at the kitchen table. I

don't think that either of them had ever seen a trick done right
before their eyes. They could not have been more amazed, and
laughed wildly in astonishment.

I retired to the daughter's bedroom to wait while they called
their mother from the living room. Lying there on Céleste's
daughter's bed, I could hear bursts of laughter and sometimes
excited voices as the call went on and on; it lasted more than half
an hour. Then I heard someone, presumably Marguerite, in the
bathroom right across the hall, getting ready for bed. When
she returned to the living room, I could hear her and Céleste
talking as they made up the couch where Marguerite would
sleep. Then I heard Céleste enter the bathroom and close the
door behind her. She was there for the longest time. I realized
that I wasn't certain what was going to happen. Maybe, with
her sister sleeping in the living room, she would go back to her
own bed, in her own bedroom. But at last she quietly knocked,
opened the bedroom door, and came to me. She was humid and
fragrant from her bath, and wrapped in a white towel.

·   ·   ·

The following morning, I happily began a life as Monsieur
Céleste. I went with her everywhere. She made her living by
giving lectures on art to many different audiences—students,
clubs, associations, members of museums, and so on. Sometimes the lectures were in a series, such as the course I had
taken, but often they stood alone on a single subject. When
a new exposition opened at one of the museums in Paris, she
would prepare a lecture on the artist, complete with slides, and
present it around the city to anyone who would invite her. I
went with her to two such events. She was very good, as she
had been during the course I took from her, clear and direct and

informed, but also gentle and charming. Her eyes wandered here and there across the audience as lights on the podium created auburn highlights in her hair. Afterward, we held hands as we walked along the Paris streets.

One afternoon, Céleste, Marguerite, and I went to the Louvre together to see the *Venus de Milo*. Since I had written a book about the statue, I could discuss it down to the smallest detail. I showed them the cracks where the different pieces are joined together, and the significant hole near her navel, now filled with plaster. That hole once held a short metal rod that supported her right arm as she reached across her body to hold up her drapery. That evening, I did card tricks for them again at the kitchen table. Céleste and I shared a last night: I had to fly back to Austin the next morning.

We had talked a little about the future. Even before a single word was said, we had both assumed that there *was* a future. But there wasn't very much that we could plan. It was the third week in August. My course at the university would begin in a few days and would meet every Monday, Wednesday, and Friday until early December, so another trip to Paris before then was impossible. She had her obligations as well, which made her coming to Austin equally impossible. So we decided that I would return to Paris right after Christmas. She would cook New Year's Eve dinner for us. After that the plans became hazy. In general, I would come live with her while she continued her life and I wrote a book. At the time, this rapidly sketched-in outline of our lives together seemed to make good sense. At Charles de Gaulle, we both agreed that short goodbyes were the best. We said a few words, and we kissed; I got out of her car and watched as she drove away.

. . .

During the long fall and winter months that followed, we wrote every day. Our correspondence became both more romantic and more filled with detail about out daily lives. She called me "mon très cher Greg" or "mon adorable Greg" and she was "Céleste, la femme de mes rêves"—the woman of my dreams—or "ma belle fleur." At the end of each message, we said we were sending kisses and tender embraces and whispering sweet words. Since her messages and my messages were in French, I spent an hour or two or even more each evening, reading her latest message and carefully composing my reply.

Careful as I was and hard as I worked, I'm sure I made many mistakes. One in particular embarrassed me when I realized what I was doing. "Coucou Greg" she wrote. If only she had put in a comma! I took that to mean something like "sweetheart Greg" or "my dear Greg." I began to use "coucou Céleste" throughout my messages. Instead, it just means "hello" or "hey, there." I hoped she would find such mistakes more endearing than annoying.

Meanwhile, I was back at the university, teaching my course and diligently working on a book I was under contract to write. She was lecturing on the Borgias and also on Hokusai, an eighteenth-century Japanese painter who was then being featured in a large exposition at the Grand Palais. She was also painting and trying to create a series of classes in which she would teach both basic and advanced techniques for painting watercolors. She even had a small exhibition in a gallery. So we were both very busy. We told each other that being busy was all for the best, since it made the time go by more quickly.

We often referred to the five days we had spent together. These
memories stayed very fresh for me, and also for her. In October, after a few days of bad weather in Paris, she wrote: "When
the weather is nice again, I'm going to go walk in the Parc
Monceau. That is going to remind me of sweet memories with
you. Time passes fairly quickly, and so I hope that December is
going to come quickly." I had already bought my ticket to leave
for Paris on December 28.

We talked about her coming to Austin after I visited her in
Paris, but she needed a new passport. She had let her old one
expire, since she didn't need it to travel in the European Union
countries and she didn't think she was interested in going anywhere else alone. But now she had a very good reason for getting a new one, and she was "going to inaugurate it in the spring
by coming to see you." That made me very happy. She often
mentioned how much she wanted to come to Austin.

But that would be sometime in the future, whereas the
date when I would come to Paris was already set and certain.
I could think only of being with her there. In mid-October,
two months since I had seen her, I wrote: "I miss you always,
but there are some days when I am able to be philosophical. I
know that our spirits are together and I know that it's only that
I have to wait and that knowledge is a comfort. But other days
I wish that I could embrace you and that we could lie together
in a bed with nothing else to do for hours. And later we would
have dinner in a corner of a café where there is good food and
good wine and where we could watch, hand in hand, the rest of
the world going by where no one knows our secret. (Or perhaps
everyone, in seeing us, knows precisely our secret.)"

And her feelings were just as strong and just as vivid: "I am
happy because you are committed to us and our future. During

our five marvelous days I felt so good with you, so happy to be with you, that what I desire most is for our history to continue. We have so much to share and to bring to each other."

We sent each other gifts. Mine was a lavishly illustrated volume about the work of Pierre-Joseph Redouté, the great watercolorist of flowers whose patrons included both Marie-Antoinette and Napoleon's wife, the empress Josephine. She sent me a bande dessinée—a fancy comic book—of Maupassant's story "Le Horla." This tale of supernatural terror is one of his most famous works. It's the account of a man going insane who believes that he is possessed by a powerful, malign spirit from another dimension he calls the Horla. Maupassant makes the bizarre events almost plausible so the story is frightening enough to read. And the drawings in the bande dessinée add significantly to the terror the story produces. I knew that she loved Maupassant, but I did wonder—just a little, before dismissing the thought—why she chose this particular Maupassant to send me.

In mid-November, she made reservations for us at a "spectacle" on New Year's Eve but wouldn't tell me what it was. It would be a surprise, although I assumed it would be nothing like the "spectacle" that Tracy and I had seen. Then we would return to her apartment for champagne, foie gras, and a chocolate bûche. Only a few days later, however, she wrote to say she was feeling melancholy and reading Dostoyevsky. I found this news very ominous. I couldn't tell if reading Dostoyevsky had made her melancholy, or if her melancholy, which had arrived for reasons I didn't know, had led her to read Dostoyevsky. I decided that the latter was more likely.

Then she wrote with even more ominous news. Her brother had called to say that their mother was so fatigued that

she hadn't gotten out of bed for two days. The next day, her
mother wasn't worse, but she wasn't better, either. She called
her mother each day after that. She wrote me and called me
"mon adorable Greg," but I had become quite worried and told
her so. Then, on December 5, she wrote that her mother had
fallen and had been taken to the hospital, unconscious. She was
flying south that morning; her brother would meet her and take
her to their mother. Several days later, she wrote to say that
her mother was out of the hospital but still suffering, and that
she herself was suffering, too. I was desolate, but not surprised,
when her next message said that it would be for the best if I
canceled my trip. I called the airline, feeling that, along with
my flight to Paris, many of my dreams were being annulled.

Her messages became sporadic after that, and the ones that
did arrive were often cold and distant as she became increasingly depressed and very bitter about love. Though she was
on good terms with her ex-husband, the fact was that her marriage had failed. And more recently, but before meeting me, she
had ended a two-year affair when her lover finally told her he
wouldn't marry her after all. Then, in the week before Christmas, she wrote a letter so warm and tender that I believed
her true self had re-emerged and we would be able to go on
together after all: "My very dear Greg, thank you for your very
kind message. I reflected a lot last night and afterward I had a
funny dream. I was with you in America and we were walking
in a forest. It was very pleasant. The forest was very dense with
gigantic trees, and then we arrived at a clearing where there
was a house like those in the north. You told me that you lived
there and you would invite me there. And suddenly there were
thousands of birds in the trees, birds very different from those
in France. They were very beautiful with magnificent blue,

orange, and green plumage. I wanted to catch them but they flew away and I wasn't able to. I was very happy to be with you, we laughed, we turned in circles around one another endlessly. I woke up and in my bed I was well, I wasn't sad, and when I was completely conscious I told myself that this dream meant something very important. I have always listened to dreams. You are a great opportunity for love for me who didn't believe in love anymore. What is happening now in my life is difficult, but I won't forget you, my Greg chéri, you are in my heart. You are a very large hope. . . . After Christmas, if Mother is better, as I so hope, we can choose some dates to see each other in January or February. I embrace you tenderly, my Greg chéri, and thank you for being there for me."

But she didn't listen to her dream. I am certain she listened to one or two other people, her psychiatrist for one and perhaps another man, and I know she listened to her depression. She sank into it completely. I don't blame her for that. I've had an attack of depression myself. You think you should fight it— in fact, you know you should fight it—but everything in your soul tells you it's useless. The darkness is stronger than you are. So I was devastated and angry but resigned when, in the middle of January 2015, she wrote that it was impossible for there to be anything between us, ever. We had been ridiculous to have ever thought it was possible. We lived too far apart, we were too different by nature and by culture, and she was depressed and didn't have the time or the will to write me anymore. My only possible reply was "As you wish." I added that someday she might change her mind, but even if that day should come, I didn't want her to write me again. And that was that.

I thought at the time, and have often thought since, and still think today, that there was more involved in this sad history than she ever told me. Her mother's trauma—assuming that really happened as she described it; sometimes I've wondered—was certainly a shock, but in her telling, that trauma made Céleste fall apart and left her completely unable to help her mother at all. It was as if Céleste were the one who had fallen. I don't want to indulge in facile psychological analysis here, but I have spent more than a few hours during the night pondering some of the obvious themes that present themselves.

I don't believe our problem was one of those deep complications caused by American naïveté confronting European manners and class consciousness, such as Henry James and Edith Wharton wrote about. I wasn't *that* naïve, I don't believe, and she was not a European aristocrat with a proud family history. In many ways she seemed American to me. She had broken with her family and become a nurse and then, by determination and talent, transformed herself into a respected teacher and artist. On the other hand, there may be something in the view of our romance as American naïveté confronting European manners. Maybe our cultural differences, originally so enchanting for us both and evidently now enchanting only for me, were the reasons why she wouldn't let me help her, and why she wanted to end things between us. But, without excluding any of the global speculations I've just made about Europe and America, the more natural explanation would not be the clash of cultures but simply the arrival on the scene of another man, someone closer by, someone who would understand every word when she whispered in his ear, someone French. She was looking for help. She would have known how to find it, and I believe she must have found it. Even so, assuming she was most likely in the arms of another, I couldn't stop myself from thinking about her.

CHAPTER THIRTEEN

Le Flâneur

Except for those final messages in January, all of 2015 passed without any contact between Céleste and me. I missed her, but there was nothing I could do about that except try to think of other things. The year before, I had signed a contract for a book about writers from Texas, which I worked on diligently; I found myself captivated by Katherine Anne Porter, a writer I had previously ignored completely. Her personai life was a shambles. All of her marriages and most of her love affairs were unhappy. She was married once to a man fifteen years younger than she was, and the unhappy couple lived in Paris for the short duration of their marriage. Paris also cropped up in the lives of other Texas writers, often in an unexpected manner. One writer's archive contained a photograph of Simone de Beauvoir standing in a bathroom, naked. As the months rolled by, I decided that, although I was missing Céleste, I was missing Paris even more, and there was definitely something I could do about that. In January 2016, I enrolled again in the language school at the Sorbonne, and spent from late January until early June in Paris.

I rented what turned out to be a large, comfortable apart-

ment in the Fourteenth Arrondissement, near the Place Denfert-
Rochereau. I hadn't told Céleste that I was coming, nor did I
write her while I was there. I thought that I might—hoped that
I might—just run into her on the street. Sometimes I would
wander by the Parc Monceau. It is always beautiful, and there is
often a lot of interesting activity there—young families playing
with their children on the swings, and art and antiques fairs on
the neighboring sidewalks. I tried to make myself believe those
were the reasons why I went there. But I never saw her, as I
hoped I would. I thought more than once about just walking
boldly down her street, although I always resisted the temptation. I knew that if I had seen her on her own street, my being
there would have been too obvious and calculated, an unwanted
intrusion.

I worked hard on the course, even while taking it rather
less seriously than I had in 2014. I was enthralled with a prin-
cesslike Korean woman who sat in front of me in class. She
always wore the latest styles, and sometimes arrived with
strands of tiny pearls woven into her long hair. Her ambition
was to become an international airline hostess. Meanwhile, I
had somehow become the friend and confidant of two young
women. Momoko from Japan and Jihyun from Korea were both
learning French because they wanted to become tour guides
in their respective countries. We sat together during lectures
and went out for dinner from time to time, Momoko knowing
exactly what to order at the Japanese restaurant we liked near
the Boulevard Saint-Germain.

But far more often I was alone, and when I was alone, Paris
beckoned to me. I began taking long, aimless walks again. I had
done much the same thing in 2014, but now I was even more
committed to these lengthy, purposeless rambles and thought

of them as defining. Three or four times a week, I set out with
the expectation that I would be gone for several hours at least.
Although I was alone, I never felt lonely. In fact, I could enjoy
the walks *only* if I were alone and free to follow my slightest
whims without the restrictions or the confinement that even
the closest friend would present. It was a way of transforming
my solitude into something I had chosen, something that was
filled with unforeseen possibilities that could never be realized
by searching for them but only by wandering and trusting to
chance.

Tracy and I had enjoyed taking long walks around our
neighborhood in Austin with our dog on a leash, but I didn't
feel her close to me during my walks in Paris, as I did in church.
Instead—and this would happen only when I wasn't thinking
of her at all—I would occasionally believe I caught sight of her
standing off to the side somewhere in the middle distance. This
sometimes happened when I climbed the steps up out of the
Métro into the sunlight; she would be in the shadows near the
top of the stairs. Or I might see her in a crowd on the other side
of the street when a noise or a flash of color made me look suddenly in that direction. In the first brief instant, I would believe
that it really was her I was seeing. It didn't seem unusual for
her to be alive and in Paris, just as it's unremarkable that she
is always alive when I dream of her. On the street, after the
instant of seeing her, reality descended, just as it does after
waking from a dream. Her apparition vanished, and I understood that she wasn't there and could not have been there. I was
left with the same feelings I would have had if I really had seen
her for an instant, only to have her disappear.

And sometimes, if the circumstances were precisely right,
those feelings swept me up even if I didn't see Tracy's appari-

tion, although such circumstances were rare. One afternoon, I walked into a hair salon near my apartment and was told that there was a woman immediately available who could cut my hair. Her name was Valérie. She was forty or so, slender and attractive, with dark hair cut just below her ears. She was wearing a pretty blue pleated skirt and a white silk blouse. I was physically attracted to her, which was a prelude to what happened a few weeks later, when I needed another haircut and went to see her again.

It was around five in the afternoon. Valérie's chair was in a small alcove just inside the door of the salon. Again she looked very attractive. She was wearing black hose and heels, a black sheath dress, and a colorful scarf knotted around her neck. She was cutting the hair of a boy about six who resembled her and had her same dark hair. A dark-haired girl of eight or nine, who had been sitting nearby, got up to ask Valérie a question about the homework she was doing. They were clearly her children. There was a pleasant, happy confusion in the air as Valérie answered her daughter's question, greeted me, and turned back to her son in the chair. I had the powerful sense that I was married to her, that these were our children in our house, and that I was arriving back home after a day at work. While my children were growing, I had had that experience almost every day, but now the children had been grown for so long that I couldn't remember the last time I had arrived home and felt that way. Was there a dead cat under the house I needed to drag away? When Valérie finished with the boy, it was my turn. I relaxed in her chair and enjoyed feeling her hands in my hair and breathing in the faint, musky scent of her perfume.

She asked me what I was doing in Paris, so I told her about taking courses at the Sorbonne and also talked about my long walks across the city. The school interested her only a little, but my walks resonated with her, because she liked long walks, too. She walked less frequently now that she had a husband and children, but she suggested several parts of Paris where I had never been that she thought I would enjoy visiting.

I hardly needed any encouragement, but her interest was a welcome validation nonetheless. So I took off for hours across the streets of Paris alone. To a degree, I was leaving Tracy behind on these walks, since so much about them depended on being completely in the present. But I was also taking her with me. The less I consciously thought about her, the more likely I was to be startled by seeing her somewhere off to the side or far ahead of me. Since I had no expectations, my walks were always completely successful and satisfying. I was never bored. What I saw was always interesting, always something that I had never seen quite that way before. The ephemeral became permanent because I was open to it, looked for it, regarded it carefully when it was before me, and remembered it. And the monumental places—the Louvre, for example, or the Place Saint-Sulpice, or the pond in the north end of the Luxembourg Gardens—became less permanent and more fluid. They presented new facets each time I saw them.

Valérie had suggested that I look around in the Fifteenth Arrondissement. Since both the shop where she worked and my apartment in 2016 were in the Fourteenth, I assumed the Fifteenth was close by. And it was, except that the border between the two arrondissements was a wide canyon with multiple railroad tracks lying along the ground like strands of twisted spaghetti. It took me longer than I expected to find one of the rare bridges across. Finally, on the other side, I found myself in an area of little interest. Stores selling building supplies were mixed among clinics and medical laboratories. I wandered south until I came to the Place d'Alleray, where, with five streets to choose from, I selected the rue Brancion, for no other reason than that it descended farther south.

An unhurried fifteen or twenty minutes later, feeling both impatient and discouraged, I brightened instantly in front of Chez Walczak, a restaurant whose walls are covered with aging photographs of boxers from the 1950s. According to a poster, Yanek Walczak had fought Sugar Ray Robinson in December 1950. In the window was a photograph of him among friends after the fight. Sitting at a table in a coat and tie, he's pulling a bandage away from a swollen black eye. Jean-Paul Belmondo was one of Walczak's friends; there's a photo of him in boxing trunks. Evidently, Walczak also knew Édith Piaf. She's in a photo with her great, doomed lover, the boxer Marcel Cerdan. And there were numerous photos and posters of Georges Brassens, the poet and popular singer of the 1950s and '60s, who lived in this neighborhood. The entrance to a large park named after him stood on the other side of the street.

I opened the door of the restaurant and entered into considerable darkness. There were long tables set along the walls, smaller tables here and there throughout, and no one at all anywhere, neither customer, waiter, nor bartender. It was about 11:30 a.m., so I presumed that the day had not yet begun Chez Walczak. I felt quite at ease being there alone. After working out at Richard Lord's boxing gym in Austin for so many years, I felt comfortable around a ring, speed bags, hanging heavy bags, and memorabilia with curling edges tacked to the walls. Here, it was as if some invisible lava had preserved Chez Walczak intact as a shrine to boxing, unchanged since 1950, like the wine shop preserved at Pompeii. I left, closing the door quietly behind me, and walked across the street to the Parc Georges-Brassens.

The park is an expanse of rolling green meadows with a large pond in the middle. Well into the 1970s, this area had been filled with fish markets and slaughterhouses, different but still somewhat similar to what Les Halles had been, which explains why there is a statue of a bull on a pillar at the entrance to the park. I walked along a hill of artificial boulders where young children were climbing and playing cache-cache (hide and seek). There was a vineyard nearby, on a hillside, and at the top I found a number of beehives, the harbinger of an important discovery later that afternoon.

Warned by the furor that arose when the pavilions at Les Halles were razed, the architects of the park preserved several structures from the old market. In a pavilion that had once served for buying and selling horses, I found a flea market devoted to rare books and magazines. I say "rare," but perhaps a better word would simply be "old." The dealers—fifty or sixty of them; the pavilion was quite large—had their stock spread out on tables or in long, sagging, temporary shelves. French movie stars from decades past, still beguiling even today, smiled at me from the covers of old magazines, while, close by, in the next stall down, heavy black type and the photos of bullet-ridden corpses blared at me from vintage true-crime publications. There were numerous copies of a Western-themed comic book called *Rodeo*, which did not seem overly concerned with accurate detail. One cover showed a cowboy wearing a fringed rawhide shirt and a broad hat. He had drawn his Colt .45 as he faced off against a gorilla.

Despite the size of the market, there didn't seem to be very many customers. Instead, the dealers talked heatedly in small groups as they bought, sold, and traded among themselves. Rare-book dealers in the United States do much the same thing. There is no pleasure for them quite like buying and selling with a peer and coming out ahead. One seller, in a corner of the market, appeared to be much younger than the rest, perhaps not even out of his teens. He had a huge thicket of filthy black hair hanging around his ears, wore jeans and red suspenders, and was insouciant to the point of rudeness. I stopped by his table because he had ten or fifteen different issues of *Combat*, the French Resistance newspaper that Albert Camus had edited. The papers were protected by plastic covers, but the seller watched me suspiciously when I picked one up. I had never seen a copy and was surprised that a Christian cross was contained in the letter "C" in the paper's logo. It couldn't have been a Christian publication, or else the atheist Camus would never have become the editor. I asked the seller about it. "Oh, the Resistance," he said, "they accepted help from anywhere." This response, though it must have been literally true, was also distinctly unhelpful. Meanwhile, he had taken the copy from me and begun gathering up the other issues, all of which he placed in a trunk, whose lid he closed, as if he were afraid I might want to buy one. Then he turned back to me with a triumphant smirk.

I left and crossed the park toward the west, and began wandering down the rue de la Saïda until I noticed that it was intersected by the Passage de Dantzig. I paused there, because I had a faint memory of wanting to see something on the Passage de Dantzig.

But the Passage de Dantzig didn't look too promising. It was literally a back alley lined with heavy green garbage bins standing by the featureless backs of buildings. Still, I wandered past the garbage bins anyway toward some greenery that was spilling over a wall near the distant end of the Passage. And that's where I found, at number 2, behind a tall, arched metal gate covered with ivy, the artists' colony of considerable legend named La Ruche—the Hive—that is now more than 115 years old. The gate, of course, was locked. It was so entwined with ivy that it must have been decades since it was last opened. The real entrance was a metal door to the right of the gate, mounted between two thick stone pillars. The door to the building was also locked, and a brass plaque on the pillar to the left said that this was private property, where visitors were forbidden without prior authorization. I would have to make do with peering inside through the ivy on the gate—which I tried, although I couldn't see much at all.

La Ruche was founded by a sculptor named Alfred Boucher in 1902. In addition to his famous tower, Gustave Eiffel had also designed a metallic structure to exhibit wine during the Universal Exposition in Paris in 1900. After the conclusion of the exhibition, Boucher rescued the materials and reassembled them as an art colony here, in what was then still a small village on the edge of Paris. The building was octagonal, three stories high, and domed, so it really did resemble a hive. Boucher also liked the name because it implied that the structure would be filled with feverish activity. This building was at the center of a large property that in time contained gardens, artists' studios, and a theater that could seat an audience of three hundred. La Ruche was a success from the beginning. It has been the home to such artists and writers as Guillaume Apollinaire, Ossip Zadkine, Marc Chagall, Fernand Léger, Max Jacob, Blaise Cendrars, Amedeo Modigliani, Constantin Brancusi, and Diego Rivera. There are several histories and memoirs concerning La Ruche.

One of interest is by the painter Marie Vorobieff, known also as Marevna, who wrote about her time at La Ruche, where she became the lover of Diego Rivera, by whom she had a daughter. In 1970, it was announced that La Ruche would be torn down, but a committee of artists and arts patrons came to the rescue and managed to save it.

I looked for several minutes at what little I could see through the ivy, and had turned to leave when I saw a group of about fifteen people walking down the Passage de Dantzig behind a stout, elderly woman who seemed to be in charge. I divined immediately that this was a walking tour about to visit La Ruche. What luck! I stood off to the side as the stout woman stopped at the metal door between two stone pillars and typed in a code she read from a piece of paper. The metal door opened, the group walked through, and no one objected when I walked into La Ruche with the tour. The grounds were a wild garden barely kept in its bed. Small sculptures, worn now by wind and rain, stood here and there amid roots and piles of rocks and staircases. One walkway led past a row of small brick buildings that doubled as studios and apartments. The doors to the hive itself were guarded by a pair of caryatids. Inside, a list of names showed that more than fifty artists were in residence. A winding wooden staircase led to the upper floors, where there were wedge-shaped apartments behind plain wooden doors. A calico cat followed us up the stairs. Everything was bright and clean and quiet, and we never saw a single person. The artists were either gone, sleeping in the afternoon, or hard at work. I prefer to presume the latter.

I left La Ruche with the tour and then abandoned them, crossed back over the railroad tracks to the Fourteenth, and wandered toward my apartment. That's how I came across the

rue des Thermopyles. This narrow passageway seems more like
a country lane than a Parisian street. It's one of the rare streets
still paved with cobblestones. Some of these had been dug up
to do repairs on some pipes underneath, but the stones themselves were carefully stacked on the side, ready to be replaced.
Wisteria hung from roofs and balconies, and must be beautiful when it blooms. At one place, a warren of rabbit hutches
extended for ten yards or so along the north edge of the street.
Handwritten signs in red and blue ink welcomed everyone to
look, assured all that the rabbits were well fed and cared for,
but implored passersby not to throw peanuts, bread, chocolate,
onions, banana skins, citrus fruits, tomatoes, or mushrooms
into the hutches, because they would make the rabbits sick.
One sign also assured us, "The rats have left." One house had
doors through whose long windows, with their delicate lace
curtains, I could see cats playing with balls of yarn beside a
rocking chair. By the time I got back home, I had been gone
almost five hours.

One sunny, warm afternoon a few days later, I decided to
take a walk down the rue Saint-Denis. The Billy Wilder film
Irma la Douce, from 1963, in which Shirley MacLaine plays a
prostitute, is set on an unnamed street in Paris that is exactly
like the rue Saint-Denis in those days. It's said that, in preparation for her role, Ms. MacLaine spent time in the neighborhood,
observing the comings and goings of women on the street.

Today the street is considerably less outré, although there
are still a handful of sex shops on it. Their doorways are draped
with filthy, heavy curtains. Inside, they sell a staggering variety of pornographic DVDs at deep discounts, but still no one
wants to buy them. The best-selling item in these shops, adver-
tised by large, hand-drawn signs on cardboard tacked on the

wall beside the heavy curtains, seems to be poppers—amyl nitrite. A popper costs ten euros. Otherwise, the street is dominated by pizza parlors, crêperies, and stores selling medium-priced, multicolored, exotic women's clothes. Their customers are either African women or goth chicks. In the store windows you see lots of black spiked high heels as well as black spiked heavy combat boots. But as I wandered toward the north end of Saint-Denis, an immensely fat woman in a black leather mini-skirt waved at me. She was standing next to a doorway covered by an iron gate, and gestured toward the doorway while rolling her eyes in invitation. Le racolage—soliciting—is against the law in France. Neither a woman nor a man may solicit either actively, by calling to passersby, or passively, by gesturing and winking, but there are certain streets in certain neighborhoods in Paris where prostitution has been present for generations and streetwalkers can offer themselves with impunity.

One of these neighborhoods is the crazy patchwork of streets just south of the Strasbourg–Saint-Denis Métro stop, where there were so many women standing by and in doorways that I felt I had entered some alternate reality. Most of the women were obese, like the woman who'd first gestured to me. I saw one grinning, muscular young man who looked like a construction worker taking the hand of a huge woman who was wearing nothing but tall black boots and a red sweater pulled down just enough to barely cover her massive behind. The two were happily going off to wherever she had her crib. Elsewhere in the neighborhood, especially but not entirely along the rue Blondel, there were women standing in doorways or just on the street. Sometimes two or three women sat on stools in doorways with their skirts pulled up and their legs spread.

Who were their customers? I couldn't imagine, although

the muscular young man who walked off holding the hand of the fat woman in the red sweater looked like a man who could have bought, or even attracted, a woman who was not grossly fat and working on the street. It fleetingly—only fleetingly— crossed my mind that perhaps he knew something that I didn't. I stifled that thought quickly.

Up ahead of me, near the corner of Blondel and Saint-Denis, I was surprised to see the back of a slender, stylish woman who seemed to be different from the rest. She wore black heels, black hose, a tailored wool skirt that wasn't too short, and a smart double-breasted jacket. From behind, she looked as if she would not be out of place working in a store that sold expensive luxury goods. But then she turned toward me, and I saw the desperate, joyless expression on her ruined face.

Back on Saint-Denis, I saw a woman working the street who confounded everything else I'd seen. She seemed to live in a separate universe, where prostitution was both exhilarating and immensely profitable. When she appeared out of nowhere, the other women on the street all gathered about to greet her. They fell into long, animated conversations. This woman was tall and slender. Her blond hair was beautifully styled, and although the temperature was almost seventy, she wore a full-length mink coat. She was walking a small dog on a leash. She had a retro elegance and extravagance, like a spoiled glamour queen of the 1950s. Soon she walked on, leaving a gaggle of streetwalkers in her wake.

France outlawed brothels in 1946, and 195 such establishments were shut down in Paris. Some—like Le Marguery, on the Boulevard de Bonne Nouvelle—were so elegant that their interiors are still preserved today. Fine "maisons closes" and exclusive procuresses may exist today—there must certainly be ways for Saudi princes and Russian oligarchs to hire expensive women in Paris—but if so, their secrets are closely guarded. Instead, those 195 brothels that existed in 1946 have been replaced by Asian massage parlors. They seem to have metastasized in the past five or six years. There is hardly a block in Paris without one. Sometimes they face each other across the street, which suggests to me that there must be rival gangs that run them, although from the outside they all look alike. I have wandered many hours around Paris, and during all that time I have never once seen a customer go into or come out of an Asian massage parlor. But, obviously, men do enter some-times, or there wouldn't be so many spas. One time, however, I happened to walk by a parlor where a masseuse was smoking a cigarette in the doorway. She was wearing a leopard-print miniskirt. As I passed by, she looked directly into my eyes with cold contempt.

From time to time, I would see aggressively elegant women on Paris streets, although the most elegant person I saw was someone I'm not sure was a woman. I saw her or him or them in the Fourteenth Arrondissement. She—I'll say "she" since that is how she presents herself—wears the most expensive clothes, including hose, gloves, and shoes, and her blond hair is combed elaborately up and back across her head. Simply getting dressed and made up must take her at least an hour. I saw her often in 2016, and three years later I saw her again, but only once. She was on a street in the Fourteenth, walking hand in hand with a short, younger man. She was wearing tight black leather pants and black shoes with tall, narrow heels. Her legs were so thin they looked like straws covered in shiny leather.

And, only a few moments later, I saw the most beautiful woman I've ever seen while I was walking nearby, along the rue Delambre. I was pondering what I was going to buy at the grocery store and wasn't on the alert to look for anything special. Since she was dressed in ordinary jeans, a simple white blouse, and white sneakers, it was as if she were venturing out into Paris incognito. I noticed her face more or less by chance and felt my stomach tighten a little, but she had already passed me before I realized how beautiful she was. I turned to look as she walked on down the sidewalk. She was slender and graceful, but from behind she was no different from many other young women. It was her face that was so beautiful. Who could she be? Her clothes seemed willfully anonymous, almost like a disguise, which made me think later that she really must be someone famous. Seeing her reminded me of both the shock and the pleasure the first time I saw Tracy, in the doorway to my office. I felt a slight, pleasant vibration that continued during the time I spent in the grocery, buying coffee, yogurt, and butter with grains of sea salt.

.   .   .

The longer I stayed in Paris, the longer my walks became. After tramping back and forth across the Butte aux Cailles, just southwest of the Place d'Italie, to see all the burgeoning street art, I wandered slowly north, all the way across Paris, to the Parc de la Villette, nourished along the way by a Vietnamese lunch at Pho Nam Bo, on the rue Baudricourt. Another day, I began at Montmartre, far in the north, and zigzagged all the way to the southern border of Paris, where at dusk I rested with a small bottle of white wine on a bench by a pond in the peaceful Parc Montsouris. I reflected on the odd whims of fortune that had led me by the rue de Tracy, just one block long in the Second Arrondissement, between Saint-Denis and

the Boulevard de Sébastopol. Slowly, I once again traversed
the Parc Monceau, lingering by the monuments to Maupassant
and Chopin, the verdant pond partially lined with faux classical
columns, the odd miniature Egyptian pyramid, and the plaque
honoring Jacques Garnerin. On October 22, 1797, he rose in a
balloon to three thousand feet over the Parc Monceau, cut the
rope that connected him to the balloon, and, in the world's first
parachute jump, descended slowly back down to the park, land-
ing shaken but unharmed. From there, I followed the Avenue
Hoche down to L'Étoile, and then kept going south across the
river to the Champ de Mars in the shadow of the Eiffel Tower.
During these walks and many others, although I had little to
show afterward but swollen ankles, I always felt that I was
accomplishing something, that I was busy, and that I was using
my time wisely.

On Christmas 2015, before I left for Paris, my family had
given me a professional-level camera that was still small enough
to fit in the front pocket of my trousers. I always had it with me
as I wandered. Back at my apartment, I would load the photographs from the camera into my computer. I began writing
accounts of my wanderings, illustrated with photographs, and
sending them to my family and friends, including my teacher
at the Sorbonne in 2014, whose husband was the comic poet.
In her response, she suggested that I read *Le Piéton de Paris*
by Léon-Paul Fargue. This title in English—*The Pedestrian
of Paris*—sounds considerably more mundane than it does in
French, but I embraced the book from the moment I started
reading it. These essays, which were first published between
1932 and 1936, are based on Fargue's restless walking around
Paris at night, in much the same way I was walking around
Paris now during the day.

Fargue had the advantage of being born in Paris in 1876 and of living there all his life until his death in 1947. He knew the city in intimate detail, through many years of experience, in a way I never can. But I felt I could aspire to his openness, his attitude, and his eye. "Myself, I am called by the secret places," he wrote in his introduction to *Le Piéton*, "also by the shadows, the sorrows, the premonitions, the smothered footsteps, the sorrows that wait behind doors, the passage of ghosts; and by the memories of old windows, of spaces, of missteps, of reflections, and of ashes of memory."

Fargue's obsessive wandering across Paris during the night was well known, and tolerated, even honored, among his friends. They knew that when he agreed to meet them for dinner he would inevitably be late, possibly hours late. He was such good company that the wait was worth it. He was a respected Symbolist poet himself and knew all the poets, novelists, painters, and composers of his day, as well as the aristocrats, society figures, and great beauties. He once had a dinner party with only two guests—Marcel Proust and James Joyce. It was the only time the two writers met.

Fargue also had his Boswell: a writer named André Beucler, a Russian noble who fled the Revolution when he was twenty and lived in Paris for the rest of his life. In Beucler's *Vingt Ans avec Léon-Paul Fargue*—the English translation is called *The Last of the Bohemians*—I found a quote from Fargue that delighted me so much that I printed it out in bold letters and taped it to the door of my office at the university. Fargue was interviewed by a Scandinavian woman who asked him about his ideas, and in particular his ideas about politics and society. He answered, "I love cats and ears, courtyards, chimneys, warm cafés on rainy days; I love folk art, the quays, cheeses, pianos, dead-end streets, wagons, does, frogs, and the beyond. So, there are my guiding principles. *Ideas?!* They are for the mediocre." The juxtaposition of cats and ears is inspired, and the rest of his list is like an inventory of Paris, assuming that does and frogs are slang for certain kinds of people one sees on the streets, possibly prostitutes and petty criminals. Unfortunately, in 1943, during the Occupation, while dining with Picasso, he was struck with hemiplegia, paralysis of one-half of his body. He survived, but he was paralyzed and forced to spend the last four years of his life bedridden, a cruel fate for an inveterate wanderer.

In reading about Fargue, I saw references to "la flânerie," which means wandering the streets of a city without a goal but open to whatever experiences might occur. The person who does this is a "flâneur." Wandering without a goal—wasn't that exactly what I was doing? I was so pleased to learn that flâneurs were a Parisian tradition, and a well-established and highly regarded literary tradition at that. Balzac—or should I say Bal*z̧ac*?—wrote: "The majority of men walk about Paris as they eat, as they live, without thinking about it. . . . Oh, to wander about Paris! Precious and delicious existence! To flâneur is a science, it is gastronomy of the eye. To merely walk is to vegetate; to flâneur is to live." Baudelaire considered the flâneur to be a highly evolved personage, as can be seen in my epigraph. He also wrote that for "the perfect flâneur, for the passionate observer, it is an immense joy to elect to reside among the many . . . to be outside your residence and still feel everywhere at home; to see the world, to be at the center of the world and remain hidden in the world, such are some of the smaller pleasures of the independent spirits." He compared the flâneur "to a kaleidoscope given conscience, which with each of its movements presents life multiplied."

I was seduced by the notion that the long walks I was taking made me a flâneur, too. Was I ever truly a kaleidoscope given conscience? I can't say, but I tried to be as hard as I could.

CHAPTER FOURTEEN

The Crèche

But when I was back home in Austin in early June 2016, I did write to Céleste after all. I made it clear that I had spent all spring in Paris without telling her that I was there, that I was now back in Austin, and that I was involved in a romance, all of which was true at the time. I told Céleste that I was describing my situation in some detail so she wouldn't think that I was hoping to resume our romance, which was not true at all. But I did admit to her that, in spite of everything that had happened, I still had tender feelings for her. Since I hadn't seen any notices for lectures by her during my time in Paris, I wondered if she still lived there, or if she had moved elsewhere. I said I would be very grateful for any news that she might send me.

I heard from her the very next day. She said that she was very happy to have heard from me and that she had wondered about me, too. She was no longer giving lectures but was completely occupied in teaching painting around Paris and at retreats in the countryside during the summer. Though she felt better, she had had a difficult year. She had no regrets but said, "When I was sick, I needed people around me and couldn't be happy with a distant friend like you in the United States, even though I understood that you would come to France from time to time. A long-distance love can never last." Her words—"A long-distance love can never last"—were very clear, but I paid less attention to them than I should have. In fact, I didn't pay any attention to them at all; I acted as if they had never been said. She concluded by saying, "When you come to Paris again let me know this time so that we can spend some time together. That would please me very much. If you wish, we can correspond. Kisses, Céleste." Those were the words I paid attention to much more than I should have.

I tried not to write her too often, but I was always looking for excuses to write her, especially when I could include a photograph I thought would interest her. When I saw John Singer Sargent's portrait of Henry James, I sent her a photograph of that, as well as a portrait of Carson McCullers by Irving Penn. And I sent her occasional family photographs. One was my three-year-old grandson playing with a deck of cards. She called him "mini-Greg." And when my romance came to an unhappy end, I told her that, too.

That's when I learned that her romantic life hadn't gone smoothly, either. The man who had been there after her depression lifted, as she put it, "decided not to really commit to me." So my suspicions were right—she *had* found another man to help her. But now she said she had a new friend. They shared a "lovely understanding" and attended lectures, expositions, and films together. I decided that this relationship wasn't really a threat to me. I should have understood that a lovely understanding was the absolute most that she wanted from me.

We continued to write during the following months. Her life as a painter and a teacher was going well. She was busy with her workshops in Paris and her summer retreats in the countryside. She sent me photographs of the former convent where she met with her students in the south, and the pretty house overlooking a long valley where she lived during the retreat. We also wrote about books. Since she was no longer lecturing, she didn't need to do the research that required, so she was free to read what she pleased. Chateaubriand's *Memoirs from Beyond the Grave* had a powerful effect on her, and she was drawn to other works about the Revolution, the Empire, and the Restoration. But her tastes ranged wide. She was enthralled by Jim Harrison—an excellent writer if a surprising choice for her, I thought. And she always seemed to be in the middle of a novel by Balzac or Maupassant.

In the early fall of 2017, I was surprised when a close friend I'd known for almost fifty years wrote that he and his wife were going to be in Paris for New Year's Eve. "Wish you could be there, too," he added. Well, I wanted to be there, too, but I told my friend that coming to Paris would be an extravagant folly. "Yes," he answered, "but no one ever regrets an extravagant folly now and then." That persuaded me; I made my airline reservations that afternoon.

And I wrote Céleste. She said she would be very happy to see me while I was in Paris. We didn't decide exactly when we would meet until much later in the year. As it happened, she left Paris around Christmas to spend a few days with her mother, but wrote me that she would be back on Tuesday, January 2, 2018. We could have dinner the following Wednesday evening. We would meet at her apartment at seven.

I had a very warm and happy New Year's Eve dinner with my old friends, and another fine dinner on New Year's Day. Then they left Paris, and for me time passed slowly until Wednesday. I resorted to la flânerie. I found that my long walks

had an added luster, and that I was particularly sensitive to the
most appealing details because of the prospect of seeing Céleste.
Wednesday night, I was unsure how long the Métro would take
to reach her apartment, so I gave myself plenty of time, and
arrived on the corner of her street at six-thirty.

To kill time, I walked around the neighborhood, which
seemed very different from three years before. Parc Monceau
was the only distinguishing feature that I remembered from
the past, but now I saw many small galleries and workshops
where solitary craftsmen made stringed musical instruments—
violins, violas, upright basses, lyres, lutes, and others—entirely
by hand. I passed a florist and—Why hadn't I thought of this
before? I knew she loved flowers!—bought a bouquet of tulips
for her. A few minutes after seven, I pressed the buzzer of her
apartment. "I'll be there in a moment," she answered. I still
had the code she had given me to open the front door, so I went
into the small lobby and waited by the elevator, which was even
smaller than I remembered. I saw the black pulleys turning and
the black cables moving as the elevator cage descended to the
floor and the elevator door opened.

Céleste emerged, smiling shyly, as she always had before.
Her head was tilted slightly to the side. I had never seen her
look so lovely. There were small hints of mascara around her
eyes, and a subtle glow on her cheeks. Her rust-red hair was
radiant and luxurious. She was wearing a smart burgundy suit
and a silk blouse. "Bonjour, Céleste," I said and handed her the
tulips.

It was clear that she had expected that we would leave for
the restaurant from the lobby and not go up to her apartment
together. But now she needed to take care of the tulips, so we
got into the elevator. Again, just as when I had first visited

Celeste, we were forced close together. We were both quiet and
tense as the elevator rose, taking care not to crush the tulips.
She opened the door of her apartment. Her cat, who had been
waiting in the short hallway, saw me and scampered away
toward the living room. After taking off our shoes, we went
that way, too. There, on a table against a wall, I saw that she
had put together an elaborate display of santons.

She started to explain, but I said, "Oh, I know what
they are. My wife loved them. Sometimes we bought them at
Georges Thuillier in Saint-Sulpice." Her arrangement was
so much like Tracy's that for a few moments I felt dislocated.
There was the stable with the crèche and the shepherd and the
adoring wise men. There was the cast of villagers in Arlesian
costumes. There was the woman with a tray of cheeses, and the
boy beating a tambourine. A stone footbridge spanned a creek
made of aluminum foil, just as a bridge had spanned the creek
in Tracy's santon village. There was a flock of sheep, a priest,
and some couples arranged as if they were dancing. A string
of cleverly hidden lights illuminated the scene in the same way
that Tracy had lit her village.

I was vibrating with associations between Tracy and
Céleste, between what I knew of the past and what I did not
know of the future, and between images in my memory and
what was before my eyes right now. Could some of Céleste's
appeal, or much of her appeal, or *all* of her appeal, come from
her similarities to Tracy, which I had recognized only uncon-
sciously? I had never thought so before, but now many similarities crowded into my mind. They both had an exquisite eye
for beauty. They both had sweet, soft voices. They both had
beautiful hair that was difficult to manage.

We went to dinner at a restaurant she had chosen nearby.

At dinner, she told me that her friend had just broken up with her, kissing her repeatedly as he did. I thought she seemed more annoyed than sad. We talked only a little about the past. I said I understood: "You needed me, and I wasn't there." She seemed to accept that, and, for my part, I didn't remind her that she had told me not to come. After we finished, the night was clear and cold, so we didn't have to run under the rain like children. Waiting on a corner for the light to change, I leaned closer to say something to her. She turned her head abruptly, thinking I was trying to kiss her. "Hmmmmm," I thought. "So that's where we stand." At her door, there was a short embrace and a friendly kiss on both cheeks. But she did send me a message at ten that evening, thanking me for our "agreeable" evening and for the pretty tulips. We had agreed to meet the next afternoon at two at the Musée Jacquemart-André.

Like the Frick Collection in New York, the Wallace Collection in London, and the Menil Collection in Houston, this museum holds a private collection of magnificent art displayed in the home of the collectors. Édouard André, the only child of a rich father and a rich mother, had inherited great wealth and became even wealthier as a banker and diplomat during the Second Empire. After the Empire fell in 1871, he left politics and devoted himself to collecting art. Nélie Jacquemart was a talented painter of society portraits who took pains to hide evidence of her obscure provincial family. They married in 1881, when he was forty-seven and she was forty. He had already built his grand house on the Boulevard Haussmann, and he and Nélie made long tours, mostly in Italy, to furnish it. When Édouard died in 1894, his cousins tried to take his estate from Nélie. She, however, had cleverly prepared a defense, and defeated the cousins in court. Today the house and the collection are preserved just as she left them, and as stipulated in her will.

The museum attracts many visitors, but usually not tourists on the large, guided tours one frequently has to dodge in the Louvre. In general, it's a calm, uncrowded place that, like the Frick, Wallace, and Menil Collections, is an inspiring and somewhat humbling monument to individual taste. I go there when I can and always take people there who have come to visit Paris. And I like the story behind the creation of the museum. Since neither Édouard nor Nélie had married until well into middle age, I assume the marriage was chaste. At any event, they had separate bedrooms in their vast house, although that may not have been unusual at the time. Chaste or not, it was a happy union of two minds, or, more precisely, two pairs of discriminating eyes. Édouard was a wealthy, Protestant, ardent Bonapartist from a grand and important family, whereas Nélie was a Catholic royalist of obscure origins. They melded together to build a great collection. Theirs was a romance of two souls who sought beauty together, and that romance has always seemed emblematic of Paris to me.

Of course, I was glad to be going there with Céleste. I had not been able to sleep the night before. At 2:30 a.m., I gave in and took a sleeping pill. That worked, but a little too well: I didn't wake up until 10:30. I ate, showered, and tried to pull myself together. On the way to the Métro, I stopped in a bookstore—one of the pleasures of France generally and of Paris in particular is that you are never far from a bookstore—and bought her a copy of *La Lenteur*—*Slowness*—by Milan Kundera. Buying her a present was an afterthought, but I was glad that I had done it. She was already at the museum when I arrived, and she was carrying a sack with a present for me.

We decided not to exchange our presents right then but to save them for later.

The museum has several rooms on the second floor that it uses for changing exhibitions. The current show was a selection of more than forty works from the collection of Wilhelm and Henny Hansen, a Danish insurance magnate and his wife, who had put together a prescient collection of Impressionist and Postimpressionist paintings in just two years, between 1916 and 1918. Among much else there were landscapes by Monet, Pissarro, and Sisley as well as important works by Renoir, Morisot, Degas, Manet, and Courbet. The exhibition culminated with a whole room devoted to Gauguin.

Walking through both the exhibition and the permanent collection with Céleste was the sweetest pleasure. She knew so much, and she looked so radiant. She showed me, for instance, how Gauguin used a certain kind of canvas to achieve various effects. It was clear when she pointed it out, but I could have looked at the paintings by myself for hours without noticing anything like that. In the permanent collection, she stopped at *The Supper at Emmaus*, which Rembrandt painted when he was in his early twenties. "It's the best painting here," she said. It's small, sixteen by seventeen inches, and shows a scene from the Gospel of Luke. Jesus appears on the evening of his resurrection to his disciple Cleopas, who has just walked six miles or so from Jerusalem to Emmaus and is eating supper. "It's the moment when he recognizes who has joined him at the table," she said. And, indeed, there is a profound expression of astonishment, fear, and wonder in the eyes of Cleopas, as well as in his open mouth, the position of his hands, and the slight tilt of his body backward and to one side. We stood for quite a long time, looking at the painting together.

The museum has a pretty tearoom with a high roof and decorative columns among the tables. When the weather is pleasant, you can sit outside, but it was January now, so we took a table by one of the columns and ordered hot chocolate. First we exchanged our gifts. She had not read *La Lenteur*. It's inspired by a novel called *Point de lendemain*—*No Tomorrow*—by Vivant Denon, for whom one of the three divisions of the Louvre is named. As she thumbed through the book and saw Denon's name, she became very excited. She was even touched, and declared that it was such a thoughtful gift. For me she had *Tous les matins du monde* by Pascal Quignard, and an anthology of passages about nature from classical French literature with a CD of the selections being read aloud. I thought they were very nice presents.

We showed each other family photos on our phones, and talked of our children and close friends, of our lives growing up, and of our work now. We stayed for more than two hours, talking all the while. I had to leave Paris in a couple of days, but I was coming back in early February, less than a month away, and we talked of all we could do together then. Our parting was Platonic—only friendly kisses on the cheek, like the night before, not even an embrace. But I didn't mind. There was nothing wrong with slowness, and that afternoon, hadn't we been our own small version of Édouard and Nélie, our spirits united by art? On the Métro back to my apartment, I thought, "This will work. No, this *is* working."

But I was wrong. I don't know what happened during the weeks I was gone from Paris. Or maybe I do know now, looking back. We kept up a friendly correspondence, often initiated by her. She sent a photograph of herself standing on a hillside in the heavy snow that had fallen on Paris. You could see her foot-

steps behind her, leading up the hill. She took a trip to Rome.
She put up an exhibition of her paintings in a café near her
apartment. I returned to Paris. We made a date for lunch, but
she had to cancel it. She was evasive about any plans for dinner.

At last, we met for lunch at the café where her paintings were
on exhibit. They were very delicate and colorful and looked
lovely against the otherwise drab and empty walls. When she
arrived, her hair was wild and unkempt, and she was dressed in
a pullover whose sleeves were unraveling in several places and
an old pair of jeans that bunched up at her waist. She seemed
willfully sloppy, as well as distracted and diffident. Whatever
expectations had animated her when we were at dinner or at the
museum after New Year's had deflated in the meantime. She
turned down the invitations I made, saying that she was just
too busy, but she did invite me to dinner one night the following
week, with a woman who had become her closest friend. Would
I bring cards and do some magic tricks?

That night, we ate not at the kitchen table but in the living room, in the dark, with our bowls of thin soup on our laps.
The friend turned out to be a dark-haired woman in her for-
ties, nicely dressed, wearing glasses with a thin black frame.
She spoke in a low monotone, almost a whisper. Often the two
of them talked between themselves, as if I weren't there. They
didn't seem to be lovers, but they did seem to be very involved
with each other. I felt that I had been invited only to provide a
little entertainment. I'm sure I was a disappointment there, too.
I hadn't been practicing any magic, and my tricks worked but
fell flat. The cat stalked out of the room as I was performing.

After that evening, we exchanged a little meaningless correspondence, but that was the last time I saw her. There was no
scene, no rupture, no last goodbye, no thanks, no best wishes

for the future, no curses, no raised voices, no anger, no excuses, no explanations, no tears. There was nothing. I suppose she had wavered slightly right after New Year's in her belief that a long-distance romance can never work, but then she caught herself. Once she reconfirmed her belief that any romance with me was useless, she saw no reason even to try. My grand Parisian love affair, a fantasy of mine since I was in high school, had barely gotten off the ground when it stalled, then fizzled for a while, and finally crashed without even a whimper. Merde.

CHAPTER FIFTEEN

Le Bal Musette

It was a year later, in February 2019, when I returned to Paris to write this book, and moved into the same apartment on the Boulevard de Port-Royal where I had stayed in 2014, during my first extended stay in Paris. I was delighted to find that Paris is a very congenial place for getting work done. Each morning, I got up, had a little fruit and yogurt for breakfast, and started writing. The apartment was always completely silent. I was never aware of anyone else in the building, except on the rare occasions when I met someone going up or down the interior stairway. I worked at the same square glass table that I had worked at when I first attended the Sorbonne. A large casement window on my left looked onto a courtyard with a small garden. I soon became used to the comings and goings of the other residents of the compound, who had to pass under my window to get to the gate on the Boulevard de Port-Royal. Around eight-thirty, there would be the kindly-looking elderly woman with short white hair, going off to her work. She always had a large canvas bag slung over her right shoulder. Around nine-fifteen, I would see the lovely violinist, with her instrument in a case strapped to her back, and I might see her again when she returned in the middle of the afternoon. She had pale skin and beautiful wheat-colored hair that she coiled on top of her head. She wore glasses in a white frame that looked glamorous on her. When I first arrived, she was always walking hand in hand with a young man, both in the morning and in the afternoon. But one day she appeared alone, and I never saw the young man again. I wondered what had happened. Perhaps I was not the only man in Paris who had lost at love. I knew that contacting Céleste was pointless. She would respond with annoyance or not respond at all.

I was completely at home in this neighborhood that I knew well from staying in the apartment five years before. Everything I needed was just a short walk away, so shopping was easier and took much less time than it often did at home. I loved the small rituals of daily life in Paris, especially the greetings when you enter a store and the farewells when you leave. In my neighborhood, the people at the store counters soon recognized me. If no one else was waiting, we would engage in brief conversations. The Algerian man who ran the little grocery across the street asked me why I was in Paris. I told him I was a writer. He was immensely curious. When he wanted to know what I was writing, I told him a little bit about this book. After that, whenever I was in the grocery, he would ask me with an air of grave concern how my work was going. I liked it; it felt good having someone completely outside my normal world pulling for me. And when I had done my quota of work for the day and needed a change or some diversion, all I had to do was go out my door, and there were all the splendors and mysteries of Paris waiting for me.

There wasn't a Métro station nearby, but there were plenty of convenient buses, which I preferred to the Metro anyway.

The 21 bus stopped catty-corner from my apartment and took me right to the door of the Louvre. The 83 bus stopped directly in front of my apartment and went diagonally across the Left Bank to the river, where it stopped near the Musée d'Orsay. As an "adhèrent" of both museums, I visited each one often. At the Louvre, I always began by going directly to the Richelieu wing to see *Milon de Croton* by Pierre Puget, a monumental statue, almost ten feet tall, in an immense, bright marble gallery containing many glorious masterpieces of French sculpture. Once or twice, I was the only visitor in the gallery, but usually there was just a small handful of other people there. The presence of such glorious art in a spacious gallery, and the absence of any crowds, make this the most appealing place in the Louvre.

At the Musée d'Orsay, there are two paintings that I always seek out first. They are on opposite sides of the museum, almost directly across from one another. Painted twenty-two years apart, they also appear to me to represent the opposite sides of a man's emotional life. The newer of the two, *Le Veuf* by Jean-Louis Forain, I've mentioned already. It is the portrait of a man in a particular moment. We see that he is a responsible man of honor, loyalty, respectability, who has felt the passion of an enduring love. The other, *Olympia* by Édouard Manet, was painted in 1863 and first shown publicly in the Salon of 1865, where it was considered an outrage. It is the portrait of a woman, but it implies a man's passion as well. Here that passion is illicit, expensive, even shameful, but also irresistible and destructively obsessive.

The woman is reclining on an opulent couch with a drape embroidered with flowers. She has an orchid in her hair, small gold earrings, a black ribbon around her neck with a small cameo, a thick gold bracelet on her right wrist, and a pair of satin pumps with short heels dangling from her feet. Otherwise she is completely nude. She is a prostitute. She is regal, luxurious, magnificent, imperious, and completely confident, but a prostitute nonetheless. And she refuses to be seen as anything else. She looks directly out of the painting at you—the viewer—and you are forced into the role of the customer for whom she has been waiting. A black maid stands behind the couch, offering her a sumptuous and obviously expensive bouquet of flowers. Perhaps you have brought it for her yourself, or perhaps it comes from another admirer. At the foot of the couch, just beyond her satin slippers, a black kitten has raised its tail, arched its back, and puffed out its fur with defiant sexuality. Even more than Brigitte Bardot in her towel, *Olympia* represents the erotic and illicit Paris of my imagination. Perhaps the blonde woman I had seen on the street in the mink coat on a warm day was her contemporary incarnation.

. . .

I had been in Paris almost two months when my brother, one of my sisters, and her husband arrived in early April, at the beginning of a tour. I took them to see Saint-Eustache, the immense Gothic cathedral near Les Halles where, as I've mentioned, I occasionally liked to attend mass on Sunday morning. It was built across one hundred years, beginning in 1532. The soaring arches in the interior are thrilling. The many chapels that surround the sanctuary contain paintings by sixteenth- and seventeenth-century masters as well as intelligently curated works of modern artists. Among other powerful works, there is a sculpture by Raymond Mason from 1971 that recalls the Les Halles food markets of the past, and a metal triptych of the life of Christ created in 1990 by Keith Haring. And it pleases me to know that Molière was both baptized and married in Saint-Eustache.

As we four lingered near the entrance, looking up at the brilliant stained-glass windows, a woman in dark glasses came in. She was wearing a brown suede hat with a wide, round brim, and had a large leather bag over her shoulder. She eyed me curiously through her dark glasses for just a moment before going on. She looked very chic beneath her stylish hat and behind her dark glasses, and I had a strong impression that I knew her somehow.

As I walked around the church with my family, I saw that she had stopped next to a thin woman wearing a white smock who was sitting in the sanctuary, drawing on a sketch pad. The woman in the hat began making small corrections to the thin woman's sketches. So she was an art instructor, like Céleste, and she was about Céleste's height and age. Could she be Céleste? I wondered. Was that why she had looked at me so strangely and yet seemed so familiar?

She left her student and began walking toward another woman with a drawing pad, who was seated on the other side of the cathedral. I walked after her quickly, and when I got close enough I called out, "Céleste?"

The woman in the hat stopped and turned to look directly at me. She wasn't Céleste. "Désolé," I said. "Excusez-moi." But even as my heart sagged and I turned away, knowing that she was someone else, I couldn't give up my belief that she really was Céleste.

Meanwhile, my sister had begun talking to the thin woman, who could speak a little English. I asked the woman the name of her art instructor, the one who was wearing the hat. "Idelette," she said. My heart sagged a second time. That tantalizing woman who had regarded me carefully for just a moment could not be Céleste after all. Or could she be? In that moment, and sometimes even now, I believe that it must have been her. She was really there, speaking softly and shyly to her students, her untamed hair hidden beneath her chic hat.

.   .   .

May 26, 2019, which happened to be Mother's Day in France, was my last Sunday in Paris before returning to Austin. My work had gone well. In addition to seeing my siblings, I had had two or three pleasant visits with friends who happened to be in Paris. I had been content living in my familiar neighborhood. But also, when I took off across some new neighborhood in Paris or revisited a museum or strolled through a familiar park, I always found something new, something unseen until then, something unexpected. My new discovery could be astonishing, or it could be simply quiet and comforting, like the chapel of perpetual adoration I found one day at the end of an obscure passageway. But my main purpose in coming to Paris had been fulfilled, and I was not sorry I was leaving. I missed my children and their families. I missed my friends. I missed my office at the university, and I missed my apartment, filled with books I loved and magic DVDs, some of which I had not yet seen. Like Tracy on her last night in Paris, I felt at last filled with Paris. I felt satiated and satisfied. I could put my arms around it all.

Fortunately, the weather that Sunday was cool and sunny with occasional gentle breezes. I walked west down the Boulevard de Port-Royal to the Luxembourg Gardens, where I turned north. With spring, the gardens had bloomed and were lush and colorful. The large pond in the north end reflected the blue sky. Children were using long sticks to push model sailboats out onto the pond. I continued on until about eleven o'clock, when I found a table at the Café de la Mairie on the Place Saint-Sulpice. Georges Thuillier, where two days before I had bought a santon for Tracy, was next door.

The Place Saint-Sulpice is dominated by a huge, hulking church, also named Saint-Sulpice. It is only slightly smaller than Notre-Dame. This church has a fraught history. Its two looming towers are mismatched, and over the main door you can still see traces of paint from the Revolution dedicating the church, not to Christianity, but to worship of a "Supreme Being." Inside, there are magnificent murals by Delacroix in the first chapel on the right, but otherwise the church gives the impression of a large, cold basement. There is a fountain in the middle of the Place. Despite the gentle weather, there weren't many people there, and even though it was Sunday, there was hardly any activity around the church.

I ordered white wine, and ham and cheese on a croissant. While I was eating, a group of about ten cyclists on the street between the café and the Place fell in line behind a leader. He shouted back to them in English, "We have only one rule." But they disappeared around a corner, and I never got to hear what the rule was. Just across the street, on the edge of the Place, I saw a tall, slender woman, quite attractive, in tight black leather pants, holding the hand of a girl about six. She kissed the man with her on the lips. It was a long, lingering kiss. The moment she stopped kissing him, he shoved a cigarette into his mouth. This deeply offended me.

On the top floor of a building on the west side of the square, on the rue Bonaparte, I could see a wall of tall windows. I'd been told at different times by several different people that Catherine

Deneuve lived there. I wondered if that was true. I also began
to wonder how long I would have to wait here in the café before
I saw someone I knew. It could be a long time or it could be five
minutes, but it wouldn't be forever. Sooner or later, someone
would happen by. I thought of Marina Abramović. In 1988, she
began walking from the east end of the Great Wall of China
and Ulay, her lover and artistic partner of many years, began
walking from the west end. By the time they met in the middle,
neither one wanted to marry as they had originally intended.
Instead, they embraced, and Marina cried, and then they went
on in separate directions to lead separate lives. I thought that
was what I should do if I passed Céleste on the street—stop,
perhaps embrace, perhaps let a tear fall, and then walk on without a word.

I ordered another glass of wine, but by the time I finished I
had grown restless. I left the café and walked across the Latin
Quarter. I passed behind the Panthéon and followed the rue
Clovis by Saint-Étienne-du-Mont to the rue Descartes, where
I turned south until it became the rue Mouffetard. I walked
by the Place de la Contrescarpe, which Hemingway describes
in the opening paragraphs of *A Moveable Feast*. I went around
the corner to see once again the building where he and his
wife, Hadley, had had their apartment when they first arrived
in Paris, in December 1921. It's a featureless but nevertheless
still comfortable-looking building, and undoubtedly expensive
today. However, in Hemingway's time, now almost one hundred years ago, this was a working-class quarter. In those days,
a man came down the street every morning, selling milk from
a goat he led by a halter.

I continued down the rue Mouffetard and passed the restaurant where the students had raised their glasses for Tracy

and me, and the thrill of feeling filled by Paris came over her. I paused there a moment to let the memory fill out and take me back in time. I felt a nostalgic, muted happiness for what once was. Alone but not lonely, I walked on to the foot of the rue Mouffetard, by the square Saint-Médard, where every Sunday there is a bal musette. The musicians may change a little from week to week, but there is always an accordion. A man and a woman sing, while another woman hands out sheets of paper with the lyrics of popular French songs from the past. A crowd comes to watch and sing, while many couples dance. A few of the couples are older. In fact, some are quite old, but, long accustomed to holding each other, they still move gracefully to the music.

I took a place at the edge of the crowd, where I could see the dancers. I wished that we had known about this tradition when Tracy and I were in Paris together. We didn't dance well or often, but when we did dance we enjoyed it, especially that night at the school in Roanne with the couple from Louisiana. We would have joined the dancers here. They were all about our age, and we would have blended right in. The last time we danced together was at Vivian's wedding, in April 2010. Everyone who was there danced, too. Afterward, I thanked the band effusively as I paid them and the leader said, "At a wedding you always play for the grandparents. That way, everyone dances." And that is exactly what had happened.

There were plenty of grandparents dancing now on the Square Saint-Médard. My muted, happy, nostalgic mood continued, and I was glad to be in Paris, listening to the music and watching the dancers on a sunny afternoon. They made me think of 2010, our last good year, when there was Vivian's wedding and the month in Provincetown and our driving back and forth between Massachusetts and Texas. We stopped along the way in Memphis, to see Graceland and to attend Al Green's church, and in Philadelphia to see the Barnes Collection, then still in Dr. Barnes's house, as he had intended. And then Tracy's cancer was diagnosed, and the last good year disintegrated into the last year.

I took a sheet of song lyrics when the woman came by and sang very softly as I watched the dancers and sank deeper into my reverie about Tracy and dancing and weddings and driving. In 2011, during the summer after her death, I drove from Austin to Provincetown again, alone this time, and did the same thing in 2012. That year, while I was driving across Ohio on my way home, I saw a sign on the road for barbecue. It was almost noon, and my stomach was empty. A few miles down the road, I saw another sign for the barbecue restaurant, pointing down a side road. I turned off. The place turned out to be farther off the highway than I had expected or wanted, but I finally saw it on the right. I parked in the dirt lot and was inside the restaurant before I realized that this was a place where Tracy and I had stopped two years before. It was bizarre and spooky, but also comforting, to be drawn blindly into this one place in a journey of a thousand miles, as if Tracy were there waiting for me.

The accordion player began a lovely waltz, and I sang along with everyone else in the square:

> *"Sous le ciel de Paris*
> *Marchent des amoureux."*

With no will of my own, but led by an invisible presence, I left the crowd, moved in among the dancers, and began to waltz by myself. My left hand was raised and my right arm was crooked, as if I were holding Tracy. Effortlessly, we stepped and swirled, stepped and swirled, stepped and swirled. When the song ended, the presence led me back into the crowd.

The musicians stopped playing at two. The dancing and singing stopped as well, and the crowd drifted away. There is a large Algerian green grocery on the square that I liked. I bought some dattes sauvages—wild dates—and ate them as I walked back to my apartment. My route led me along the rue Claude-Bernard, past the building where the young couple and their toddler had lived when, in May 2013, I first heard about the language school at the Sorbonne. I stopped and looked through the locked metal grill that covered the door to their building. Six years ago, I had walked through that door and climbed five flights of stairs to the apartment of strangers. There, without expecting it and without knowing at the time what was happening, I picked up my life again and filled it—as I had that morning in Saint-Sulpice and that afternoon at the bal musette—with Paris.

Acknowledgments

I owe debts, both great and small, to everyone mentioned in this book, and to my family in particular. Thank you, one and all.

But I am also grateful to several people who are not mentioned. My close friends Stephen Harrigan and William Broyles were encouraging from the moment I first admitted that I was thinking about writing a book about Paris. It was Steve who gave me the title. Having that question settled early on guided me as I thought through what the book would be. Both Steve and Bill read and commented on my original proposal, and then both of them read my completed manuscript and made extensive valuable comments and suggestions. Their help made this a better book. My agent, David McCormick, was enthusiastic from the beginning and handled placing the book with his usual skill and efficiency. Ann Close at Knopf has been my editor since 2000. Here, as with my previous books, her guidance and belief in my work have been essential, and I am eternally grateful.

A NOTE ABOUT THE AUTHOR

Gregory Curtis is the author of *The Cave Painters: Probing the Mysteries of the World's First Artists* and *Disarmed: The Story of the Venus de Milo*. He was editor of *Texas Monthly* from 1981 until 2000. His writing has appeared in *The New York Times*, *The New York Times Magazine*, *Fortune*, *Time*, and *Rolling Stone*, among other publications. A graduate of Rice University and San Francisco State College, he lives in Austin, Texas.

A NOTE ON THE TYPE

Pierre Simon Fournier *le jeune* (1712–1768), who designed the type used in this book, was both an originator and a collector of types. His services to the art of printing were his design of letters, his creation of ornaments and initials, and his standardization of type sizes. His types are old style in character and sharply cut. In 1764 and 1766 he published his *Manuel typographique*, a treatise on the history of French types and printing, on typefounding in all its details, and on what many consider his most important contribution to typography—the measurement of type by the point system.

Composed by Digital Composition, Berryville, Virginia
Printed and bound by Berryville Graphics, Berryville, Virginia
Designed by Maria Carella